MONEY SEX & POWER

Collins Enyeribe

 EFI Publications

MONEY, SEX AND POWER
Imitating Jesus Christ

ISBN 978-978-083-774-7

First Published in 2014 by

EFI Publications, a division of
Evangelical Fellowship Institute Inc.
www.evangelicalfellowshipinstitute.org

Contents

SAYINGS OF THE WISE

"Money and time are the heaviest burdens of life, and…the unhappiest of all mortals are those who have more of either than they know how to use."
Samuel Johnson

"There are two powerful drives in the lives of men and women which the devil has used to trap them and put them in bondage. They are the drives to remain alive and have sex." Dr. D. K. Olukoya

"Let us more and more insist on raising funds of love, of kindness, of understanding, of peace. Money will come if we seek first the Kingdom of God – the rest will be given."
Mother Teresa

"I don't think it is a sin to be rich, it's a sin to die rich."
Rick Warren

"Material things are a shadow. You can never find God when in pursuit of material things. If however you are pursuing God, not only will you find God and everlasting joy, you will have material things you never struggled for." Pastor E. A. Adeboye

"Riches usually make one wretched and miserable. One spends forty years accumulating his wealth and the final thirty years keeping others from getting it." Jack van Impe

"I believe that it is anti-Christian and unholy for any Christian to live with the object of accumulating wealth."
Charles H. Spurgeon

[Source: Microsoft® Encarta® 2009. © 1993-2008]

Part One

DESTINY

1

WHAT IS DESTINY?

Then Jesus said to His disciples. "If anyone desires to come after Me. let him deny himself, and take up his cross, and follow Me. ... For what profit is it to a man if he gains the whole world, and loses his own soul? Or what will a man give in exchange for his soul? For the Son of Man will come in the glory of His Father with His angels, and then He will reward each according to his works."
Mt 16:24-27

BIBLICAL DESTINY

Most English language dictionaries equate destiny with fate, fortune, luck, lot, circumstances or portion. The biblical concept of destiny must begin from recognizing that God created all things and mankind for His purpose and pleasure. God created Adam, male and female, in His image and likeness. The image of God in man is eternal life or Hypostatic Chip, as I prefer to call it. When Adam was created he had a Hypostatic Chip in his spirit. When Eve was separated from Adam she equally had her separate Hypostatic Chip. The plan of God was that people should come into the world implanted with Hypostatic Chip at conception. This was not to be because Adam transgressed the commandment of God and died in a spiritual sense. However, Jesus proceeded from the Father and came to earth to recover and restore what God lost. Those who believe in Christ's substitutional death on the Cross of Calvary can receive a Hypostatic Chip at the point of regeneration. This is where destiny fulfillment begins.

There can be no destiny without purpose. Jesus came into the world to pay the price for sin. Therefore, going to the Cross to die was part of His destiny (Jn 18:37). Your purpose is determined by who you are. Who you are is a function of where you came from, what you do regularly and where you are going afterwards. You cannot know where you are going if you do not know where you came from. If you are born of God, you came from heaven above and will return there, all things being equal.

THE MAN GOD CREATED

The original design for man is not a trinity of spirit, soul and body. The physical body was not created but formed from the dust of the earth. The innerman or inward personality comprising spirit and soul was created simultaneously with dual function in relation to the physical and unseen realms. To be complete as a person and function as originally designed by God, one must be infused with a Hypostatic Chip. The Holy Spirit performs the function of transforming a person to be like Christ through the instrumentality of the implanted Chip.

Your destiny is inscribed in your Hypostatic Chip. This was done by God a long time ago, even before the earth was created. Therefore, your destiny is God's purpose for your life, that is, your appointed or ordained future, what God has pre-determined you to be before you were born by earthly parents. It is also the expectation of heaven for your life, that is, what was written in heavenly records concerning you: what God had in mind when He created you and allowed you to come into this world. The destiny of Jesus was inscribed in the scroll of the book. "*Then I said: 'Behold, I have come – In the volume of the book it is written of Me – to do You will, O God'*" (Heb 10:7). Every believer's destiny was written in the volume of the book before the foundation of the world (Eph 1:3-4). Destiny fulfillment is God's desire for His children.

2

THE THREE MUSKETEERS

*"And you shall remember the Lord your God,
for it is He who gives you power to get wealth,
that He may establish His covenant which
He swore to your fathers, as it is this day.
Then it shall be, if you by any means forget
the Lord your God, and follow other gods,
and serve them and worship them,
I testify against you this day that
you shall surely perish."*
Deut 8:18-19

A FRIEND OR AN ADVERSARY?

The term 'Musketeer' was used to describe an infantryman armed with a musket, a member of a company of the French royal household's personal troops in the 17th and 18th centuries.

"The Three Musketeers" is a novel (1844) by French writer Alexandre Dumas. Set in France during the reign of Louis XIII, this historical romance tells the story of a young adventurer, D'Artagnan, who is taken under the wing of three musketeers, Athos, Porthos, and Aramis. The four become embroiled in a series of adventures involving love, politics, swordsmanship, and the machinations of the evil Cardinal Richelieu.

There are five characters in this novel. D'Artagnan a young adventurer can be likened to a young Christian pilgrim. Cardinal Richelieu, an evil genius, can be likened to Satan in his role as the hinderer of pilgrims' progress. The three musketeers in the human situation are Money, Power and Sex. The interaction between these three as dictated by the spirit behind human activity, God or Satan, determines man's rising or downfall.

The life of a Christian is motivated by Christ and His love. The life of an unsaved person is motivated by the desire to live long, enjoy sex and the pleasures of this present evil world. He knows that   he needs money in order to have access to pleasure. The easiest way to have money is to have power, whether political, economic, spiritual or social such as entertainment and sports. Power comes from two sources: God or Satan. Thus unregenerate humanity is driven by power for money and pleasure of which sexual indulgence is its most eloquent exponent.

God gives man power to make and enjoy wealth. The entrance of sin in the world corrupted God's design for power, money and sex. Satan uses the corrupt version to blindfold, pollute and bind people in demonic fetters that lead to perdition.

Power   =   Holy Ghost power
          =   Satanic power

Money   =   Righteous prosperity
          =   Unrighteous mammon

Sex   =   Divine pleasure
          =   Deceitful pleasure

In human interaction three phenomena stand out: power, money and pleasure. Power is needed to acquire money in order to enjoy pleasurable pursuits especially sex. The modern 'musketeers' are power, money and pleasure expressed mostly in sexual gratification. There is a spirit behind each one of them. The three musketeers are active in the world today and will become even more active as the return of the Lord draws nearer and nearer. That is because everyone needs power, money and sensual pleasure. Virtually everyone uses power and money to prolong life and enjoy sex.

Nothing is free on earth. Divine gifts require accountability. Everyone will be tested and tempted with what was done or not done regarding bestowed money, power and pleasure. Jesus was tempted on all points as we do yet He did not sin. Jesus is the standard of God. Everybody will be judged on what was done or not done in the area of money, power and sexual indulgence.

Everyone will be rewarded or punished regarding quest for power, acquisition and utilization of money, and involvement or otherwise with sexual pleasure. Jesus is judge of the dead and the living. When He returns to earth with the rapture of the church He will judge everyone's involvement with power, money and pleasure according to God's divine standards.

The vast majority of mankind spends most of their time thinking about money and sex and power for more money and more sex and much more power for limitless supply of money for endless sensual pleasure. It is a vicious circle: the desire for power, money and sex has no terminal point except with cessation of physical fitness. As much as King David loved women he was unable to relish the sexual fervors of young and beautiful Abishag in his old age. King Solomon described the inordinate pursuit of power, money and sex as "*vanity and grasping for the wind.*"

Two of your most valuable God-given assets are time and talents. Time is a wasting asset. The way you spend your time is a clear indication of where you are going in life's journey. Your attitude to time can be measured by what you pay attention to. If you spend your time with the wise, you will become wise. Spend your time with people who can affect your life positively and you can become a success yourself.

Talents are bestowals of capacity from God. They are tradable assets, but must be discovered to be used. God who gave you talents expects stewardship dues from you.

In the final analysis your life is the composite of the role played by, and the interrelationship between, money, power and pleasure vis-a-vis the utilization of time and talents in determining your success or the lack of it, which ultimately will determine your eternal destination. Human activity is driven essentially by MONEY, SEX AND POWER.

Part Two

MONEY

... in the Scroll of the Book it is written ...

on
MONEY

"For you know the grace of our Lord Jesus Christ, that though He was rich, yet for your sakes He became poor, that you through His poverty might become rich." (2 Cor 8:9)

"And Jesus said to him, 'Foxes have holes and birds of the air have nests, but the Son of Man has nowhere to lay His head.'" (Mt 8:20)

"And He said to them, 'Take heed and beware of covetousness, for one's life does not consist in the abundance of the things he possesses.'" (Lk 12:15)

3

MONEY

Then Jesus looked around and said to
His disciples, "How hard it is for those who
have riches to enter the kingdom of God!"
Mk 10:23

WHAT IS MONEY?

Money is a means of exchange, a legal tender generally accepted as payment for goods and services in a country or an economic bloc. Money as a token of exchange and money's worth are acquired when time and talents are applied into productive use for profit. The Bible has a lot to say about money: *"For wisdom is a defense as money is a defense"* (Eccl 7:12). Also, "a *feast is made for laughter, and wine makes merry; but money answers everything"* (Eccl 10:19).

Your purchasing power is a measure of your life. Life is in the blood. The way you utilize your purchasing power determines your level of success or failure in life. Many people spend their money frivolously. As purchasing power, money bestows the capacity:

1. To acquire the world's goods and services without limit.

2. To control means of wealth and use it for selfish or unselfish purposes.

3. To live in security and safety without fear of sudden terror.

4. A state of not being in want of anything money can buy.

Money is not only purchasing power it is a weapon of war in the kingdom of God as well as the kingdom of darkness. Satan uses it to empower his children to steal, kill and destroy what belongs to creation by derailing human destinies. God uses it to empower His children to build a legacy of eternal heritage in time and eternity.

Time is money. Your money is your blood measured in terms of time spent in acquiring things of value. Life is in the blood. Your blood can be accounted for by your resources represented by money or money's worth by expending your life over a period of time. When you spend money gained through legitimate labor, you are spending your blood. When you spend your blood, or rather money on things connected with the mandate of Jesus, you receive the blessing of God with no sorrow attached to it. See Mt 6:33. When you spend your life-blood money on an ungodly cause, it attracts God's curse with closed heavens and eternal wrath if not repented of before physical death.

Money as purchasing power intrinsically is neutral being neither virtuous nor evil. In the hands of an undisciplined person, money has the power to corrupt absolutely. Politicians and operators in the three tiers of government have checks and balances to curtail the corrupting influence of money in social and national life. The equivalent of that in Christian ministry is the voice of the Holy Spirit for those who choose to obey Him.

MONEY AND PROSPERITY

Real prosperity is the offspring of righteousness. Money in the hands of a righteous person can produce prosperity. God's desire is to make man righteous through Jesus Christ. The planting of a Hypostatic Chip in the human spirit is the beginning of righteous prosperity. Without this mini-God being in control of the innerman purchasing power cannot be acquired and utilized in a righteous manner. Even in benevolence, motive can be corrupt. It is a contradiction in terms to have a righteous sinner.

MONEY AND RIGHTEOUSNESS

Money is not the principal thing. Wisdom is. Jesus is the wisdom of God. Wisdom is to know and do the will of God per time. It is good to have plenty of money. It helps in solving a lot of human problems. Lack of money is a harbinger of destruction; it can cause people to die before their time.

Men love power. Money has power. Men worship money because they love power. Power is needed to gratify the lusts of the eyes and flesh. Without power, pride of life is subdued to insignificance. The desire to have purchasing power is the root of all the evils in the world.

Money is not synonymous with riches. It is possible to have money without being rich. To be rich means to have abundant wealth. Purchasing power acquired by righteous means satisfies the soul. God is the source of true riches. God gives the power to become rich without sorrowful effects. The wealth of the world is ephemeral. The riches of Christ are eternal. The world was created by Christ for His pleasure. To be rich without Christ is to be extremely poor. Poverty of the spirit is worse than poverty of material things.

The spirit of the world, which energizes the love of money, ensures that no one ever has enough money. Those who have too much money are greedier for more of it. The pursuit of money will always lead to destruction. Study the lifestyle of Hollywood stars and learn a lesson from the way they end their lives. Many rich people are servants of money. The love of money is the foundation of sorrow. Many rich people are living empty sorrowful lives.

When wealth comes into the hands of the righteous, it is for a purpose. Failure to ascertain what that purpose is and fulfill it can lead to trouble. The blessing of the Lord that brings riches is not always in monetary terms. Talents differ from person to person.

True wealth resides in God. For everyone born into this world, God has made a provisional allocation of a Hypostatic Chip, which is part of Himself. Wealth must be used for God's business for it not to dissipate. Unless a person has a proper relationship with God, riches can be misused and lead to destruction. Destruction is not annihilation, but change in form from good to bad, or from bad to worse. God is everywhere present, but He must be sought diligently to be found. Without God, material things do not count. The power of having too much money results in the searing of the human heart. Those who have sold their hearts to making much money do enjoy the good things of this life but eternal reward awaits them in the lake of fire, unless they repent before physical death.

In real terms a person is measured by the thoughts of his or her heart rather than the abundance of material things he or she has acquired or the lack of it. *"Finally, brethren, whatever things are true, whatever things are noble, whatever things are just, whatever things are pure, whatever things are lovely, whatever things are of good report, if there is any virtue and if there is anything praiseworthy—meditate on these things"* (Phil 4:8). Whoever or whatever you think about most of the time has a controlling influence over your life. Whatever draws your attention most of the time has the power to control you.

Individuals, families and nations have been destroyed for lack of money. In the same vein, individuals, families and nations have been destroyed because of too much money. Children of the rich are ruined because of too much money. Children of the poor perish for lack of it. Therefore, do not destroy your children with idle wealth or abject poverty. Strive to maintain a good balance. *"Remove falsehood and lies far from me; give me neither poverty nor riches — feed me with the food allotted to me"* (Prov 30:8).

The promises of God are for those who put their trust completely, not partially, on Him. Those who assiduously seek after money and things can get them, without God. You cannot add God to things. When a person seeks God diligently and finds Him, God adds things by giving power to make wealth. *"And you shall remember the Lord your God, for it is He who gives you power to get wealth, that He may establish His covenant which He swore to your fathers, as it is this day"* (Deut 8:18).

Envying the wealth of a sinner is idolatry. Covetousness has become a besetting sin that does not look like sin because through gradualism it has come to be accepted as normal. Gradualism is closely associated with repetition. It is the principle of one step at a time. The first step may be imperceptible. Diligent application of pressure leads to the second step. Many people have committed avoidable sins due to peer pressure. Heinous infractions of God's law sometimes take a long time to mature.

Repetition is the principle that it is easier to repeat a sinful act than get involved in it the first time. A Christian does not have the habit of committing sin, but once he or she falls into it, and does nothing quickly to achieve restoration, he or she can easily fall into the same sin again and again. The spirit of repetition will then begin to harden the heart over that particular sin until the level of "it does not matter" is reached. Many people including Christians indulge in it. It is expressed mostly in "get-rich-quick" schemes. Christians who play lotteries are covetous. What you have not labored for can bring you sorrow. The blessing of the Lord in response to the works of our hands never does.

Money, riches, wealth and poverty are things of the mind. Man is not naturally endowed to be content with money and material things. The inter-personal commandments God gave to man are intended to curb man's propensity to be enslaved by money.

1. Honor your parents.
2. Do not murder.
3. Do not commit adultery.
4. Do not steal.
5. Do not lie.
6. Do not covet.

Human beings need "things" physical and emotional. As purchasing power, money is required to acquire things. Therefore, human beings spend a lot of their time thinking about money and how to acquire it. Things can be acquired through God or without Him. Wealth acquired without God brings sorrow. The wealth God gives has no sorrow; it brings contentment, peace and joy.

The world's method of 'enjoying life' is to acquire things of value. Wealth becomes the object of living. But the Lord's method of bestowing wealth is to seek the kingdom and righteousness of God. Worldly wealth is not always corruptly acquired. God rewards hard work. The spiritual law of sowing and reaping works for everyone who keys into its tenets. What makes wealth worldly or godly is the state of the heart of the possessor. Wealthy people pride themselves for their ingenuity. Godly people, with or without stupendous wealth, look up to God as their source of benevolence.

MONEY AND WISDOM

Ungodly people are accustomed to laying treasures on the earth. Earthly treasures shall come to an end one day. Earthly treasures can diminish in value with time, canker, rust or be stolen. Ungodly treasures exist only in the physical domain. Treasures of godly people exist in time and eternity.

Wisdom is more important than money and power. I have come to realize that the greatest challenge confronting great men and women of God is in the area of money, sex and pride. Devices to camouflage weakness in these areas usually do not last long. Attempts to cover-up with excessive zeal in the worship of God are futile. Failure of church leaders always brings reproach to the entire Body of Christ. Why do men lust for things and thereby love money?

Covetousness

The root cause of the love for money is covetousness – wanting to have more and more. Intense desire to have 'things' breeds lust. It operates in three spheres: lust of the eyes, lust of the flesh and the pride of life. In many communities the value put on people is determined by the things they have.

Fear

Human desire is to live long, enjoy the good things of life and be respected as a person in society. Fear is rooted in 'what if' syndrome.

Fear of faces. What will people say?

Fear of fences. There may be insufficient knowledge to justify one's assumed position. This can bring shame.

Fear of the future. Evidence of low persuasion in what one believes. This is an aspect of lack of faith. It is the harbinger of discouragement.

Fear of failure. Suppose the expected results do not manifest in the end? What are failure results?

Worry. This is the opposite of faith.

Money does not always satisfy. Lust is never satisfied but only assuaged for a brief period of time. Covetousness brings discontentment. Men do terrible things to have money in order to enjoy and preserve life. But all to no avail. The body that is being gratified is nothing but painted mud. The body is kept alive by blood. Sin is in the blood. The corrupting power of sin in the blood makes the body to decay and die.

Flesh and blood cannot inherit the kingdom of God. Money cannot keep the body alive indefinitely.

LOVE OF MONEY

The love of money is common to both the rich and the poor. To be rich is not evil; to love money is. Love is reserved for God and fellow human beings. It is possible to have plenty of money without being prosperous. Joseph was a slave in Potiphar's house and later went to prison through wrong accusation. The verdict of heaven: "*The Lord was with Joseph, and he was a successful man; ... and showed him mercy, and He gave him favor in the sight of the keeper of the prison*" (Gen 39:2,21).

It is possible to have little money and be prosperous. What determines wealth is not the quantum of what one has but the state of one's heart and lifestyle. The heart follows treasure and what you love is determined, not by what you do or do not have, but by who you are. It is possible to be wealthy in material things and not love money or be attracted away from God because of it.

Money is not the root of all evil. It is the love of it that is. Money is amoral. Why do wealthy people covet more riches than the poor? The fear of 'what if?' Why do poor people steal to make ends meet? Because of fear as already explained. For the rich and poor, fear is responsible for the love of money.

If you earn a living from salary, and look up to your employer as your source, you can easily be controlled by the power of money. People who do what they are created to do are easily contended. Contentment does not come from money but from rendering useful service to mankind. Contentment is of the heart, not of 'things' that can easily divert from destiny pursuit. The principle of the world is fear and self-will. The result is worry. Worry is the absence of faith and without faith, it is impossible to please God.

ENSNARING POWER OF MONEY

Money acquired in unrighteous manner leads to wicked prosperity. Prosperity can be wicked; it can be righteous. Wicked prosperity ends with the using on earth. The rich man in hell received his good things in life but in hell he was tormented. Righteous prosperity endures forever.

Making money is not the same as creating wealth. You can have money without being wealthy. You can be rich without being fulfilled. Wealth in the hands of the wicked is a destroyer. There is no disappointment so cruel like the failure of money. Those who trust in riches are the poorest people on earth.

Satan gives wealth but takes it away with interest at the most inauspicious time. The wealth of the wicked always tends to poverty. Wealth acquired in an unrighteous way gives temporary pleasure. It is impossible for ill-gotten gain not to exact a degrading fee down the heritage line. Those who love God and His children are the richest people on earth.

4

MAMMON OF UNRIGHTEOUSNESS

*"And I say to you, make friends for yourselves
by unrighteous mammon, that when you fail,
they may receive you into
an everlasting home."*
Lk 16:9

RIGHTEOUS AND UNRIGHTEOUS MAMMON

Mammon is a term signifying worldly possessions acquired and utilized under the influence of the god of riches who is typified as *'the ruler of the darkness of this world,'* being infernally opposed to the 'riches *of the glory of Christ's inheritance in the saints.'* Unrighteousness in mammon stems from whether it is earned legitimately or illegitimately, legally or illegally, morally or immorally.

Mammon has bewitching, corruptive and destructive power hence the love of money is the root of all kinds of evil in the world. Wealth used to gratify human lusts ends with the using by providing temporary pleasure. The human body it is used to adorn will ultimately return to dust which is Satan's food. The riches of Christ and Satan's unrighteous mammon are so diametrically opposed to each other that the love of one automatically excludes the love of the other. As it is written: *"No one can serve two masters; for either he will hate the one and love the other, or else he will be loyal to the one and despise the other. You cannot serve God and mammon"* (Mt 6:24).

You cannot love God and mammon contemporaneously. *"And I say to you, make friends for yourselves by unrighteous mammon, that when you fail, they may receive you into an everlasting home"*(Lk 16:9).

WHY JESUS DESCRIBED MAMMON AS UNRIGHTEOUS

The unrighteousness of mammon stems from three angles: how it is earned, how it is used and its inherent corruptive, captivating and destructive power. It is human nature to love money and what money can do. Men deploy their best effort to have money and use it for self-gratification.

Acquisition

Money is neutral. It can be acquired legitimately or illegitimately, legally or illegally, morally or immorally. When money is earned by a laboring person as wages, it is good money. When the same cash enters the hands of a prostitute as the price of a dog, it becomes filthy and unrighteous. The world pursues money for power, glory and pleasure.

Utilization

How money is used determines its usefulness in time and eternity. When used for God it creates treasures in heaven where moth cannot eat it. When used on self:

1. It ends with the using. Moth eats what is not used eventually.

2. It creates treasure for earth. The human body it is used to gratify will ultimately return to dust, which is Satan's food according to Gen 3:19 and Isa 65:25. The human body of saints and sinners alike will covert to dust at death and will be burnt by fire after the White Throne Judgment with the debris deposited in the lake of fire to fuel the eternal fires of Geheena.

3. It is a doorway for bewitchment. The love of money is the root cause of avoidable human tragedies. As it is written, "*For the love of money is a root of all kinds of evil, for which some have strayed from the faith in their greediness, and pierced themselves through with many sorrows.*" 1 Tim 6:10

When the world's treasure is acquired judiciously and used wholly to serve God and His purpose for planet earth according to the mandate of Jesus, mammon becomes an instrument for creating treasures in heaven where it cannot be wasted. However, if mammon is acquired according to the principles of this world, hoarded or expended on worldly pleasure it ends with the user creating treasure for earth.

In the first of the Ten Commandments God said "*you shall have no other gods before Me.*" Mammon says make riches the god of this world your god. Jesus summarized the Ten Commandments by saying: "*You shall love the Lord your God with all your heart, with all your soul, and with all your mind. This is the first and great commandment. And the second is like it: You shall love your neighbor as yourself. On these two commandments hang all the Law and the Prophets*" (Mt 22:37-40). The god of this world says love money and all it has to offer. Have a good slice of it; this life is all that you have. The gospel of unrighteous mammon is the opposite of the Ten Commandments. It encourages people to be "*lovers of themselves, lovers of money, boasters, proud, blasphemers, disobedient to parents, unthankful, unholy, unloving, unforgiving, slanderers, without self-control, brutal, despisers of good, traitors, headstrong, haughty, lovers of pleasure rather than lovers of God*" (2 Tim 3:2-4).

SERVANT OF GOD OR CAPTIVE OF MAMMON

Every responsible adult on planet earth is a servant to God or mammon, the god of riches. You cannot serve both at the same time. Mammon which represents riches, worldly goods and services and anything that has the attribute of gain in the eyes of the beholder is typified by:

1. Worldly excitement in sports, pastime and extracurricular activities.

2. Personal sense of satisfaction in acquiring chattels and immovable properties for self-gratification.

3. Anything that excites the lust of the flesh, exemplified by unscriptural sexual pleasure and penchant for exotic food to gratify the belly.

4. Pride of life in doing and achieving what others are unable to attain.

5. A life of ease.

6. Over-indulgence in sleep and pleasure.

7. Preferment for public approbation and the praise of men.

8. Power of control over other people.

9. Pre-occupation with self.

As a Christian your income is your life. Your life is in your blood. Life on earth ebbs with the passage of time and the time you spend earning an income is the measure of your life you have put in it. Therefore the way you spend your money is a pointer to your owner. You cannot spend most of your income on worldly things and claim to belong to Christ. There are four things that belong to the church-age believer:

1. The present joy of entering heaven.

2. Prizes that Jesus will distribute at the Judgment Seat.

3. Membership of the Priesthood with the privilege of ruling the earth with the Lord Jesus Christ for 1,000 years.

4. The prospect of dwelling in the New Jerusalem in the presence of the triune God eternally.

Broadly, there are two classes of people on earth: those who are serving God wholeheartedly and those who are serving self on the platform of the world system of greed, force and corruption. Jesus said: *"No one can serve two masters; for either he will hate the one and love the other, or else he will be loyal to the one and despise the other. You cannot serve God and mammon"* (Mt 6:24). You serve Jesus by surrendering all to Him or nothing at all. The two options are mutually exclusive: love God or love the world.

> Lk 16:8-13 (NLT
> **"The rich man had to admire the dishonest rascal for being so shrewd. And it is true that the citizens of this world are shrewder than the godly are. I tell you, use your worldly resources to benefit others and make friends. In this way, your generosity stores up a reward for you in heaven. Unless you are faithful in small matters, you won't be faithful in large ones. If you cheat even a little, you won't be honest with greater responsibilities. And if you are untrustworthy about worldly wealth, who will trust you with the true riches of heaven? And if you are not faithful with other people's money, why should you be trusted with money of your own? No one can serve two masters. For you will hate one and love the other, or be devoted to one and despise the other. You cannot serve both God and money"**

The marginal note on Luke 16:9 says "*Then when you run out at the end of this life, your friends will welcome you into eternal homes*" (NLT). The expressions 'hereafter,' 'when you fail' and 'when you run out' are references to old age, sudden illness, accident or the proverbial rainy day. The wisdom of this world is to make provisions for the unexpected in the days when the body begins to grow weak and feeble.

What is a Christian's 'hereafter' and how does he or she make preparations for it? The unbelievers' hereafter is in this world. The Christian's hereafter is not in this world. Thus, material things, good life, death and dying are not of concern to the believer in Christ Jesus. The life of a Christian is deemed hidden in Christ and in God. Consequently, the wealth of a believer belongs wholly to the Lord and should be cast upon many waters. *"Cast your bread upon the waters, for you will find it after many days"* (Eccl 11:1).

'Waters' is a reference to people. In this case the Body of Christ made up of people, poor or rich as well as unbelievers to bring to Christ. The wisdom of this world is for unbelievers to put their wealth in fixed deposit accounts in local and foreign banks for interest, buy land for capital appreciation, invest in funds and business to increase wealth through high-yielding returns. It is not wrong for a Christian to acquire wealth through those means. A believer must realize that since no one can receive anything except it has been given to him from above, the wealth that accrues to a Christian is given in trust for the purpose of building everlasting legacies in heaven not here on earth. In that respect, it must be noted that:

1. Mammon of unrighteousness is a reference to things that belong to this world and must go the way of this world if not properly invested in eternal securities.

2. Happiness derived from the wealth of this world is always short-lived: there must be an end.

3. At death or rapture *'the tree lies where it has fallen'* which means that the Lord has a day to reckon with each and everyone one of us.

Unfaithfulness in the use of the things of this world to serve the master disqualifies from getting the real treasure needed to build an eternal habitation in heaven. There are only two acceptable ways for a Christian to spend his or her money or money's worth in order to be equipped to trade for real riches. Personal and family necessities of life are part of serving God. A married man who neglects to take care of his family has denied the faith being an infidel.

The second is the mandate of Jesus, which is to seek and save the lost in order to re-establish the kingdom of God on earth. The mandate contains every believer's divine assignment and it is the duty of the believer to ascertain what it is and pursue it with the world's unrighteous mammon in his control.

Fruits are grown but gifts of the Spirit are given. Without the gifts it is impossible to grow the fruits and without fruits grace can be forfeited. Therefore the riches of this world are important for the work of God but not as important as the grace that follows proper application of the world's wealth ceded to someone. The mite woman who gave her entire livelihood to God qualified for abundant grace to receive spiritual gifts for more fruitfulness in this life and true treasures of heaven.

Unrighteous mammon attracts eaters, thieves and must be protected to avoid dissipation. Besides, it must be left behind at death for known or unknown people to enjoy or destroy. With money and material possession we must be good stewards of the bounties we are blessed with. It is dangerous for a Christian to be wealthy without knowing how to deploy his or her wealth for the service of the Lord after making due allowance for legitimate needs. I believe Paul had that in mind when he said: "*But those who desire to be rich fall into temptation and a snare, and into many foolish and harmful lusts which drown men in destruction and perdition*" (1 Tim 6:9). We are therefore warned:

1. To shun hypocrisy in our use of the mammon of unrighteousness.

2. Resist the temptation to covet the material wealth of this world.

3. Refuse to make our earthly belongings rule over us.

4. Take proper decisions regarding our treasure.

5. Ensure that unrighteous mammon does not lead us to forfeit the glories of heaven.

6. Choose who to serve: God or unrighteous mammon since it is impossible to serve the two masters at the same time.

The treasures of the earth will return to origin, namely dust. True treasures in heaven last forever. Eternal life and destiny are embedded in every believer's Hypostatic Chip. The greatest treasure in this life is to have one's name written in the Lamb's Book of Life (Lk 10:20). There is a difference between laying up treasure on earth and laying up treasures for ourselves in heaven.

The acquisition of heavenly treasures follows a process:

1. Translation from death to life.

2. Proper handling of the Word of God.

3. Conscious setting of affections on things above and not on things below.

4. Walking with diligence the narrow path that leads to heaven.

5. Acceptance with God, that is right-standing at all times. (1 Tim 6:9)

Everybody on planet earth must choose the master he or she wants to serve: God or mammon, which is worldly treasures. Working out one's salvation with fear and trembling and storing up treasures in heaven are two sides of the same coin. Your store of treasure in heaven is useless to you if you do not qualify to be evacuated to heaven at the appointed time. If you do not use your material resources to build eternal treasure in heaven but qualify to dwell in heaven, when you get to there you will realize the great loss and cry when it is too late to turn things around.

Therefore, work your way to heaven and at the same time build eternal treasure in heaven with your time, talents and material wealth. Do not neglect either of them. Above all, make sure you qualify to participate in the rapture of the church as a living or sleeping saint. It is better to be a door-keeper in heaven than to neglect saving grace and at last languish in hellfire.

5

DECEITFULNESS OF RICHES

*"Now he who received seed
among the thorns is he who hears
the word, and the cares of this world and
the deceitfulness of riches choke the
word, and he becomes unfruitful."*
Mt 13:22

Money answers to all things good and evil: it is a wall of defense to the possessor. *"The rich man's wealth is his strong city; the destruction of the poor is their poverty"* (Prov 10:15). Money is needed in destiny fulfillment; it can be used to store treasure in heaven where corruption cannot touch it. Money can be used to buy vice and work against God and His plan for planet earth.

The power of money flows from the spirit behind it. The spirit of mammon is the god of riches. It is the same spirit that brought divine curses on man and creation and introduced corruption, wickedness and depravity in the human situation.

THE SPIRIT BEHIND HUMAN DEPRAVITY

There is a spirit behind every activity in the world. The two spirits at work in the world today are the Holy Spirit manifesting through those who have received Him. *"Now we have received, not the spirit of the world, but the spirit which is of God; that we might know the things that are freely given to us of God"* (1 Cor 2:12). This is the spirit of truth that governs the lives of those who are not of this world. There is another spirit. It is the spirit of the world. Those who operate with this spirit are of the world. The Holy Spirit is a person. So also is Satan who is the spirit of the world. He is the prince of the power of the air, energizing and controlling the children of disobedience.

The spirit of the world thrives on wickedness. The desire to have money, power and enjoy sex is its harbinger. Wickedness could be in character, conduct, or speech. Wicked spirits operate through human beings. Persons possessed by wicked spirits are witches and wizards. In my place of birth, for instance, the villagers take delight in killing one another through remote control. It is written: *"The heart is deceitful above all things, and desperately wicked: who can know it?"* (Jer 17:9).

In Gen 6:5, it is recorded that God regretted creating man because of his wickedness. Being a God of a second chance, God gave Noah's family, after the destruction of the old world by a flood of waters, the same mandate He gave to Adam. Wickedness resurfaced. The people developed a mind-set to disobey God. Idolatry reigned. Then God bypassed the Gentiles and chose Abraham for a seven-fold blessing.

The deceitfulness of riches is that it produces wicked prosperity through bewitchment. The wickedness of the wicked is to reject light and grope in darkness for present reward. Money is the fuel for wickedness. Hence the love of money, the inordinate desire to acquire more and more of it in order to excel in wickedness is the root of all evil. "*But those who desire to be rich fall into temptation and a snare, and into many foolish and harmful lusts which drown men in destruction and perdition. For the love of money is a root of all kinds of evil, for which some have strayed from the faith in their greediness, and pierced themselves through with many sorrows*" (1 Tim 6:9-10).

Characteristics of wicked prosperity – Ps 73:1-19:

1. Faithlessness. No God-kind of faith. Rather, poverty of faith prevails.

2. Not looking up to Jesus.

3. Love the world more than God.

4. May prefer to remain here and enjoy his or her wealth even after completing course rather than fall asleep and go to heaven.

5. May despise 'poor' brethren.

6. Exhibit Pharisee syndrome and disdain genuine seekers.

7. Friend of the world: friendship with God's enemies is enmity against God.

8. Heart will be drawn to wealth rather than to God. "*For where your treasure is, there your heart will be also*" (Mt 6:21).

9. Unprofitable steward: not using what God has provided to do God's business.

10. Likely to miss the rapture of the church.

11. Die unprepared for heaven.

One big problem with material wealth is that it has the capacity for diverting attention from the real issues of life. Money, like strong drink, gives temporary relief from spiritual poverty. People do incredible things for money. The love of money is covetousness which is lust, the desire to have. It is at the root of all the evils in the world. Worldly things can posses their owners and take them to the place appointed for the earth and its contents – destruction by fire. "*The fool has said in his heart, 'There is no God.' They are corrupt, and have done abominable iniquity; there is none who does good.*" (Ps 53:1). Those who misuse and abuse this world attract the wrath of God. "*God is a just judge, and God is angry with the wicked every day.*" (Ps 7:11). The wicked are those who have no relationship with the Lord Jesus Christ and lovers of pleasure more than lovers of God.

God is not against the acquisition of wealth. To be rich is not a sin. In fact, God is delighted when people acquire and use wealth in a righteous manner. To be poor is not good either. Poverty is not always caused by sin. Rather, it is the result of ignorance, lack or neglect of opportunity and laziness. God did not bring poverty into the world; the transgression of Adam did.

Abraham, the father of faith, believed God and it was accounted unto him for righteousness. God called him "friend" – a rare privilege. Abraham was very rich. God takes pleasure in the prosperity of His servants. Job "*was blameless and upright, and one who feared God and shunned evil.*" With one wife and ten children, Job was extremely rich and the greatest of all the people of the East. God boasted about him to Satan in heaven and Job got into serious battle of faith in consequence. He lost everything. He overcame Satan and his hordes and received double for all that he had lost. One of the most remarkable statements made by Job was: "*I know that my redeemer lives.*"

Wealthy people use their riches to acquire things of value, including good health. Poor people resort to prayer and faith. When the woman with the issue of blood pent all her money and did not get better but rather grew worse, she took the risk of being stoned to death by touching the helm of the garment of Jesus. It was unlawful for her to do so. Jesus saw her faith. Rather than condemn her, He commended her for her trust in God. The problem with riches is it detracts from saving faith. If a person can provide for himself all that he needs what need is there in believing for a miracle? Trusting in riches is idolatry.

The deceitfulness of riches stems from the following facts:

1. The trophies human beings strive to accumulate over a lifetime are perishable commodities. Their usefulness ends in this life.

2. A man's life is not measured by the quantum of things acquired because they are ephemeral.

3. What a man thinks of himself and what the public thinks of him are irrelevant and useless in the final analysis. It is what God thinks about a person that counts both in time and in eternity. Only God has the power to kill or make alive.

4. When Jesus returns to take possession of the earth, the topography of the earth will be so altered that it would be impossible for any survivor of the tribulation wrath of God to lay claim to any piece of landed property because the "*cities of the nations shall fall*" (Rev 16:19).

5. The memory of the wicked shall perish. The titles, national and international honors, spectacular records created in politics, sports, music and other human endeavors shall vanish. The only memories that remain are good deeds that attract eternal rewards from God the Father and God the Son.

Abundant Life

Jesus said: "*... I have come that they may have life, and that they may have it more abundantly*" (Jn 10:10). Idle wealth is not evidence of abundant life. Being stupendously rich or walloping in chronic poverty do not fit into the abundant life Christ died on the Cross for. Excessive wealth not deployed for the benefit of God and mankind can magnetize the heart away from God. It is extremely difficult for a person to be stupendously rich and be focused on things that have eternal value without being baptized by the Holy Spirit. You cannot be baptized by the Holy Spirit unless you are genuinely born again and desire the gift. You cannot be born again unless you have been convicted of sin by the

Holy Spirit at the hearing of faith, the gospel of the grace of God which is the power of God that beings salvation.

It is impossible for riches not to possess the heart of one not under the control of the Holy Spirit. For the righteous, the Hypostatic Chip is the invisible link connecting him or her with the Holy Trinity. For the unrighteous, the occupying demon is the link to the satanic kingdom. Wealth has bewitching power. The combination of satanic deception, cravings of the flesh and the world system of greed and avarice makes is easier to trust in riches than to trust in God.

Although God blesses His children on earth, Christ's true riches are reserved for those who love God in heaven. What are true riches?

1. To be reconciled to God through translation from death to life.

2. To receive the gift of eternal life resident in implanted Hypostatic Chip.

3. To have the God-kind of faith in order to run the race successfully to the end.

4. Contentment with godliness.

5. Heaven consciousness.

6. Destiny fulfillment.

7. Rapture-readiness.

8. Expected end in heaven.

... in the Scroll of the Book it is written ...

on **SEX**

"But I say to you that whoever looks at a woman to lust for her has already committed adultery with her in his heart. (Mt 5:28)

But fornication and all uncleanness or covetousness, let it not even be named among you, as is fitting for saints. (Eph 5:3)

For we do not have a High Priest who cannot sympathize with our weaknesses, but was in all points tempted as we are, yet without sin. (Heb 4:15)

Part Three

SEX

6

WHY GOD CREATED SEX

And the Lord God said, "It is not good that man should be alone; I will make him a helper comparable to him."
Gen 2:18

ORIGIN OF COITION

In the beginning when God created man sexual intimacy as we know it today was not part of his make-up. God made man male and female in one entity called Adam a living being created in His image and likeness. The male and female components of man were present in Adam – Eve was inside Adam.

Before Eve was formed from one of Adam's ribs, Adam and Eve had one spirit, one soul and one body. With his spirit, Adam had access to the unseen world, the domain of God. With his soul, Adam had control over his physical body which related with the visible world, the domain of mankind, through five senses of seeing, hearing, smelling, tasting and touching. His physical body is the housing for his innerman, comprising soul and spirit which are invisible to the human eye. His body gave Adam legitimate right of occupation of earth. "*Then God saw everything He had made, and indeed it was very good*" (Gen 1:31).

Before Eve was made a separate entity, Adam was a hermaphrodite. He did not lack reproductive power. God commanded Adam to replenish the earth. Meanwhile God took Adam and put him in living quarters, gave him His Word to test his loyalty to Him and an occupation to keep him busy and gainfully employed. Adam did his job well but "*there was not found a helper comparable to him*" (Gen 2:20). From Adam's perspective something was missing – companionship. "*And the Lord God said, 'It is not good that man should be alone; I will make him a helper comparable to him'*" (Gen 2:18).

God saw that Adam lacked companionship whenever He was not around for fellowship in the cool of the evening. God was eager for Adam to succeed in fulfilling his destiny; he needed a helper and an encourager. God did not say He would make Adam a child bearer. He made a help 'meet' suitable and comparable to him. God never makes mistakes. Gen 2:21-25 – the rib of Adam was used to develop and form, not create, Eve. All human beings were deemed created simultaneously with the creation of Adam, in the similitude of 'completely-knocked-down' (CKD) parts.

PURPOSE OF SEX

God designed sexual intimacy to complete the production process by involving His children in marital relationship in an exercise so enjoyable and second only to being in the presence of the Lord Jesus Christ.   The innerman, comprising spirit and soul, were created simultaneously with the creation of Adam. Just as the body of Adam was formed with 'dust of the ground' marital conjugation is the process that forms the body that houses the innerman. With Eve separated from Adam, God removed attribute of hermaphrodite and created sex as a way of forming human bodies to house innerman and Hypostatic Chips. God made sex beautiful for both Adam and Eve. Libido was designed to excite sexual desire in Adam and Eve principally for companionship and participation in bringing sons of God into the world in an exciting and enjoyable way. God did not create heterosexual sex for childbearing but as a concomitant part of it. The earth could have been refilled without separating Eve from Adam.

Before Eve was taken from Adam she lived in Adam. The separation brought two spirits two souls and two bodies. The spirit is housing for Hypostatic Chip. Coition reunites the souls with body and spirit. It is a godly soul-tie the only avenue for expressing agape-love.

Sexual intimacy is an exchange of tokens. In marriage both man and woman have tokens. When a male sex organ, in the process of penetrating the female birth canal, breaks the hymen, a thin mucous membrane that covers the opening of the birth canal, blood flows touching the male organ. The blood is the female's token of virginity while semen deposited in the birth canal is the male's token of marriage, a blood exchange. This blood covenant creates a soul-tie. Even where tearing of the hymen is not the case, the flow of blood is assumed, because sexual intimacy is a blood covenant. Marriage joined by God must be man and woman without previous ungodly soul-tie. Sexual intimacy was designed for companionship in marriage.

God's original design for coition within marriage made provision for one man, one woman who meet the prerequisites, and leaving and cleaving of the man and the woman to become one flesh. Coition is the divine method for joining a man and a woman in marriage. The first sex act is a bonding blood covenant which is the seal of marriage. The two persons become one flesh, a joining of two souls in the spiritual realm. It is either godly or ungodly.

In Gen 1:28 God told Adam to *"be fruitful and multiply."* Fruitfulness comes before multiplication. Fruitfulness means fruit of the Spirit, children in the Lord, those begotten through the gospel and brought into the Church of Jesus Christ: this is usually the result of personal evangelism and the preaching of the Gospel message. Others are fruit of one's hands acquired through obedience to the Word of God, fruit of the womb, a reference to biological children, and fruit of the lips, praise and thanksgiving. Sex is the oil that lubricates fruitfulness, not just childbearing. God desires the earth to be refilled with godly offspring. Fruitless couples usually produce godless children. The earth cannot be refilled in this dispensation. Destiny fulfillment is the principal thing. Marriage is honorable. The marriage bed is the home medical centre for husband and wife. Hence, the primary purpose of sex is cleaving, which is the closest approximation to companionship. God created sex to enable man fulfill his divine destiny.

CORRUPTION OF SEXUAL INTIMACY

God performed matrimonial ceremony between Adam and Eve by bringing Eve to Adam as his bride but Adam was not joined to his wife as a son of God. This first human marriage was incomplete. Adam and Eve had not 'cleaved' before the appearance of Satan in the form of a serpent to tempt Eve. It was after the temptation and fall that Adam *'knew Eve his wife'* an euphemism for sexual intimacy. Thereafter, Adam and Eve cleaved to each other in an ungodly manner. Adam had become a son of the devil when he knew his wife and became joined to her in an ungodly soul-tie.

The first act of sexual intimacy between a man and a woman is the seal on their marriage. It is a blood covenant. Outside the bound of marriage, such an act creates an ungodly soul tie. Sexual intimacy between a man and a woman outside biblical marriage creates an ungodly soul-tie that results in fragmentation of souls. Also, coition outside godly marriage is a sin committed inside the human body, which is the temple of the Holy Spirit – an abomination before the Lord. Marriage without heterosexual sex is not regarded as wedlock in heaven making same-sex marriage an abomination: it is sexual perversion.

SEXUAL PERVERSION

The world has perverted sexual relationship. Advocates of humanistic philosophies say you can:

1. Indulge in sex for pleasure.

2. Avoid the responsibilities of motherhood and fatherhood with the use of contraceptives.

3. Where mistakes occur, correct them through abortion.

4. Shack-up without the 'inconvenience' of procreation; that is, avoid having biological children within the design of family life.

5. Marriage has become obsolete, therefore, do what pleases you; your body is all you have.

6. Where your national law does not permit polygamy and polyandry, then marry and remarry as many times as you desire.

7. Same-sex marriage is the exercise of your fundamental human right.

It is believed in many quarters that the body of a woman is only flesh meant to be enjoyed and discarded at will. It is not surprising that the biggest industry in the world today is perverted sex. It is everywhere. It is the engine that drives virtually every aspect of human activity: governance, commerce, industry, sports and education, it is all there. Remove sex from the human agenda, or rather, put sex in its proper perspective and covetousness will be reduced by more than ninety percent. Misuse of sex is a gross abuse of God's creative power given to man.

Sex is a powerful force in the world today. It has always been. Apostle Paul's counsel to the unmarried is *"if they cannot contain, let them marry: for it is better to marry than to burn."* Sexual intimacy is the oil that lubricates the engine of marriage. It is the divine duty of the woman to make herself attractive available and pleasurable to her husband. It is the divine duty of a husband to give his wife sexual satisfaction.

DANGERS OF UNLAWFUL SEXUAL INTIMACY

1. Unplanned pregnancy.

2. Ungodly soul-ties.

3. Transmission of sicknesses through evil spirits of infirmity.

4. Demons are passed from one person to another through sexual immorality.

5. Sexually transmitted diseases (STDs), which include the dreaded HIV-AIDS.

6. Destiny truncation.
    1) Loss of inheritance – Reuben.
    2) Diversion of destiny – Judah, Samson.
    3) Wars – Schechem
    4) Perversion of justice – Herod and Salome on John the Baptist.
    5) Rejection of the Gospel – King Agrippa and Bernice.
    6) Death – Zimri & Cozbi, Ammon, Absalom.
    7) Whoring Israelites at foot of Mt Sinai.
    8) Civil war in Israel – Levite and his concubine
    9) King David and Beersheba – temporary loss of throne.

MAMMONISM AND SEX

The drive for power and money is essentially to gratify the appetite for sex and sensual pleasure. The first act of sexual intimacy between a man and a woman outside biblical marriage creates an ungodly soul tie that results in fragmentation of lives. Conjugal sex is serious business. Dowries, bride price, priestly declarations cannot make a man and a woman one flesh. Conjugal sex does. Man, created in the image of God is a partaker in creation. This is done through sex within marriage and the spoken word. When God said *"Be fruitful and multiply, replenish the earth"* He meant with godly seed. At that time Adam and Eve were sinless.

Ultimately, the desire for money and power is to have unlimited access to sexual lusts. Power brings money, especially political power and money brings sensual pleasure of which sex is the most gratifying aspect. Show me a man who has overcome the desire for sexual lust and I will show you a man on his way to heaven.

SEX: GOD'S LOVE GIFT TO MAN

Almighty God the Creator of things visible and invisible designed sex for man-woman companionship in marital union. Also, He designed sex to enable His children participate in human creation. There are other reasons God created sex, but the primary purpose is companionship. This is because Adam with Eve inside of him was a hermaphrodite with the capacity to reproduce his kind and refill the earth. Marriage is honorable and the undefiled matrimonial bed is the vehicle for the free-flow of agape love in marital relationship. Sex is God's gift of love to His children hence it is not for frivolous amusement. It is so sacred that engaging in it for fun attracts serious divine penalties. The expectation is that the undefiled bed will produce the Remnant that will repopulate the earth after the Day of the Lord.

Since God created sex as an instrument of companionship, it follows that marriage is sex and sex is marriage. Sex outside marriage is abomination; marriage without sex is a contradiction in terms. In addition to companionship, God created sex:

1. As a means of bonding souls of a man and a woman in marital relationship: soul-tie is the supernatural means of tying two souls with coition.

2. As a catalyst for the functioning of agape, a foretaste of Trinitarian agape.

3. As the acme of enjoyment foreshadowing the joyful relationship between Christ and His Church.

4. As a mechanism of defense against satanic attack in the matrimonial union. A godly soul-tie is the greatest protection against marital breakdown.

5. As a means for man made in the image and likeness of God to experience the creative power of God in obeying the command to replenish the earth with holy offspring.

For those with the gift of celibacy or who have made themselves eunuchs for the sake of the kingdom, and those who have chosen to be single, abstaining from human marriage and sex is a foretaste of the peculiarity of rapture-participating saints who shall be like angels in glory. "*Jesus answered and said to them, 'You are mistaken, not knowing the Scriptures nor the power of God. For in the resurrection they neither marry nor are given in marriage, but are like angels of God in heaven'*" (Mt 22:29-30).

Sexual intimacy is good within marriage. Sexual sins exclude offenders from heaven. In this life it is good to marry to avoid the sin of fornication and adultery. Abstaining from coition except in a godly soul-tied marriage is noble. That is why every form of ungodly matrimonial relationship must be broken by those serious about making it to heaven. The matter of relationships deserving of divorce and dissolution has been dealt with extensively in our book **DIVORCE AND REMARRIAGE, What The Bible Teaches** and need not be repeated here for space.

7

SEX AND THE BELIEVER

*It is good for a man not to touch a woman.
nevertheless, because of sexual immorality, let
each man have his own wife, and let each woman
have her own husband. Let the husband render to his
wife the affection due her, and likewise also the wife to her
husband. The wife does not have authority over her own body,
but the husband does. And likewise the husband does not have
authority over his own body, but the wife does. Do not deprive one
another except with consent for a time, that you may give yourselves
to fasting and prayer; and come together again so that Satan does
not tempt you because of your lack of self-control. But I say this as a
concession, not as a commandment. For I wish that all men were
even as I myself. But each one has his own gift from God, one in this
manner and another in that.*
1 Cor 7:1-7

WHO IS A NEW COVENANT BELIEVER?

Of the three groups of people on earth today, the Bible has concluded Jews and Gentiles under sin.

> Rom 3:21-24
> **But now the righteousness of God apart from the law is revealed, being witnessed by the Law and the Prophets, even the righteousness of God, through faith in Jesus Christ, to all and on all who believe. For there is no difference; for all have sinned and fall short of the glory of God, being justified freely by His grace through the redemption that is in Christ Jesus"**

All that come into the world are born spiritually dead destined for the lake of fire. The new birth is a change in destiny and destination. It is attained through repentance, restitution and deliverance from evil inheritance and incubated satanic deposits in the body. To be born again according to Jn 3:3, 5 means translation from death to life, ability to see the basic nature of things from the perspective of heaven and the power to be on the narrow road to heaven.

To become a Christian is to accept by faith the substitutional work of Christ on the cross of Calvary. As it is written "*as many as received Him, to them He gave the right to become children of God, to those who believe in His name: who were born, not of blood, nor of the will of the flesh, nor of the will of man, but of God*" (Jn 1:12-13). The believer is a new creation imbued with the divine nature and implanted with a Hypostatic Chip, the Incorruptible Seed from the heart of God (Ps 82:6).

A Christian must grow in grace per time. A non-growing Christian is a liability in the Body of Christ. Regeneration takes place at a point in time. It is passive. Renewing the mind is a continuous process; from regeneration to call to glory. It is an active force that must be fuelled with the Word of God in order to grow to maturity and perfection. Regeneration is to be followed by exploring the riches of Christ in the implanted Hypostatic Chip in the power of the Holy Spirit. It essentially involves hearing, reading, studying, meditating and doing the Word of God.

The new covenant saint who is growing in grace is God's ambassador to the earth, and like a pilgrim, is in the world but not of the world. According to 1 Pet 2:9-10, a Christian belongs to the chosen generation, royal priesthood, holy nation, and peculiar people. Their primary assignment is to worship God and do His bidding by showing forth His praises on earth. At the fullness of time they will be evacuated to heaven to be united with the head of the Church, the Lord Jesus Christ and be with Him forever.

THE ROLE OF SEX IN GOD'S KINGDOM

From the beginning of creation God made man male and female in one entity called Adam a living being created in the image and likeness of God. *"Then God saw everything He had made, and indeed it was very good"* (Gen 1:31). God commanded Adam to replenish the earth. Meanwhile God took Adam and put him in living quarters, gave him His Word to test his loyalty to Him and an occupation to keep him busy and gainfully employed. Adam did his job well but *"there was not found a helper comparable to him."*

Gen 2:21-25
And the Lord God caused a deep sleep to fall on Adam, and he slept; and He took one of his ribs, and closed up the flesh in its place. Then the rib which the Lord God had taken from man He made into a woman, and He brought her to the man. And Adam said: "This is now bone of my bones and flesh of my flesh; she shall be called Woman, because she was taken out of Man." Therefore a man shall leave his father and mother and be joined to his wife, and they shall become one flesh. And they were both naked, the man and his wife, and were not ashamed.

This was the first human marriage, but it was incomplete. Some time elapsed between the nuptial wedlock and the appearance of Satan in the form of a serpent to tempt Eve. Adam and Eve may have 'left' God their Father and Mother but had not 'cleaved' at this time. It was after the temptation and fall that Adam 'cleaved' to Eve his wife and harvested ungodly soul-tie and a fragmented life. Sexual intimacy is the divine method for joining a man and a woman in marriage.

Mk 10:5-9
"And Jesus answered and said to them, because of the hardness of your heart he wrote you this precept. But from the beginning of the creation, God made them male and female. For this reason a man shall leave his father and mother and be joined to his wife, and the two shall become one flesh; so then they are no longer two, but one flesh. Therefore what God has joined together, let not man separate."

The Bible makes it clear that what God has joined together should not be put asunder by man. Human marriage recognized in heaven is one sealed with sexual intimacy. If a man and a woman exchange marital vows but refuse to engage in conjugal sex, no marriage has taken place. The implication is that every act of sexual intimacy is either a confirmation of an existing marriage or the contracting of a new one. The two become one flesh. It does not matter the circumstances under which the sex act was performed, a union has been formed. The two have become one body in the spiritual realm. It is either godly or ungodly.

Coition is like the signature and seal on a commercial contract, meal eaten when cutting a covenant or the fire that went through Abraham's covenant sacrifice that signified the marriage of Israel to Jehovah. From God's perspective, sexual intimacy is a sacred gift to humanity for participation in creation. Its misuse kindles the wrath of God because of the negative effect it has on the spirit, soul and body of the persons involved as well as the Body of Christ. *"Every sin that a man does is outside the body, but he who commits sexual immorality sins against his own body"* (1 Cor 6:18).

THE ROLE OF SEX IN HUMAN INTERACTION

Marriage is joining and sex is the apparatus used to bring it about. God is involved in godly soul-ties. That is why what God has joined together should not be put asunder by man. The corollary is that any marriage not joined by God is an ungodly soul-tie – an abomination to God.

Consequently, there is no 'free' sex. It is either biblical or otherwise, resulting in positive or negative reward. It is not fun. Rather, it is serious business – the all-important business of destiny fulfillment.

As a man if you say 'I am having it with my legitimately married wife' then you must love her to the point that you are willing to die for her just as the Lord loved the church and gave Himself for her.

As a woman, if you say 'I am having it with my legitimately married husband' then you must be so submissive to your husband to be relevant in his life and not be spewed out just as the church is irrelevant without her head the Lord Jesus Christ. An irrelevant 'church' is easily spewed out of the presence of the Lord. Even so a spouse who becomes a whoremonger has become irrelevant in the marital union.

If you have it with another's spouse, you have done folly, provoked the land and the avenger of blood will not rest until you have paid the price with your own blood for sinning against your own body and defiling the marriage that God instituted for the benefit of those who obey Him.

If as a man you defile a virgin and abandon her, you have humbled a person created in the likeness of God and will be required without repentance to be cast in the lake of fire on the last day as a whoremonger.

If as a woman you offer your body for 'fun' or money to a man you are not married to you have thrown something that is holy to the dogs and will reap misery in this life and condemnation in the life to come unless you repent and receive forgiveness from God and cleansing by the blood of Jesus.

If as a man you have it with a harlot you are entitled to receive up to 49 demons from that single act. "The moment the man commits sin with a prostitute, demons from the last seven men who had sex with the prostitute automatically gain entrance into his life" (Dr D. K. Olukoya). In addition, having sex with a harlot creates a doorway for evil spirit spouses. "When people come together sexually in an illegitimate way ... doctors tell us that each person would in effect have been sleeping with the last seven sexual partners of either person. If any of the last seven people transmitted any disease to one partner, the other would get it" (Emeka Nwamkpa). According to Rebecca Brown "demons are a venereal disease."

Incest, homosexuality and corrupt sexual practices such as pornography always lead to demonic infestation. Demons and demonic bondage are either inherited or acquired through sexual immorality. Unbiblical sex is the occasion for the exchange of evil spirits supervising witchcraft and occult covenants from one person to several others most times without their being aware of it. Hence the divine admonition is "*do you not know that he who is joined to a harlot is one body with her? For 'the two,' He says, 'shall become one flesh.' Flee sexual immorality. Every sin that a man does is outside the body, but he who commits sexual immorality sins against his own body*" (1 Cor 6:16, 18).

SEX WITHIN GODLY MARRIAGE

In this end time getting involved with marriage by Christians should be regarded as a privilege, not a right. Perilous times are here already, wickedness is multiplying exponentially and the return of the Lord is imminent. Therefore, "*It is good for a man not to touch a woman*" (1 Cor 1:1). When Jesus reinstated God's original plan for marriage by telling His disciples that "*Whoever divorces his wife and marries another commits adultery against her and if a woman divorces her husband and marries another, she commits adultery*" (Mk 10:11-12) they were shocked. "*His disciples said to Him, "If such is the case of the man with his wife, it is better not to marry."* Jesus explaining what He meant told them that it was better to seek the kingdom of God without marital entanglement. The reward is greater than the inconvenience.

> Mt 19:12-13
> **"For there are eunuchs who were born thus from their mother's womb, and there are eunuchs who were made eunuchs by men, and there are eunuchs who have made themselves eunuchs for the kingdom of heaven's sake. He who is able to accept it, let him accept it."**

Those who have the gift of celibacy and those who can discipline themselves against sexual immorality should avoid marriage. However, there is no sin in getting married, except that married people should obey biblical rules on marriage and contend with problems inherent in marital union. Apostle Paul's counsel is:

> 1 Cor 7:7-9
> **"I wish that all men were even as I myself. But each one has his own gift from God, one in this manner and another in that. But I say to the unmarried and to the widows: It is good for them if they remain even as I am; but if they cannot exercise self-control, let them marry. For it is better to marry than to burn with passion"**

Apostle Paul did not say if you want to have children then marry. Rather he said that it is better to marry to quench the fires of lust. The purpose of marriage is to have legitimate sexual intimacy and avoid fleshly distraction from destiny pursuit. Libido is not meant to be suppressed except you have the gift of celibacy like Paul. Ministers of God who claim taking an oath of celibacy will prevent them from committing sexual sins are deluding themselves. Sexual sins are committed in the heart. When a man is 'burning' inside, his bed is easily defiled.

When two people are joined in matrimony without premarital sex, the first conjugal act binds them with a godly soul-tie. Subsequent sexual intimacy is the oil that lubricates the engine of marriage. As already observed, it is the divine duty of the woman to make herself attractive and available to her husband just as it is the divine duty of a husband to give his wife sexual satisfaction at all times. A woman can dishonor the marriage bed by showing no interest in love-making with her husband.

There is a difference between love-making and having sex. When a woman grudgingly allows the husband to have sex with her, she is defiling the marriage bed; she is not ministering to the needs of her husband and the union can develop marital complications. A defiled bed can lead to lack of answer to prayer. Since the primary purpose of sex is companionship marriage is honorable as the platform for its expression. Therefore, the undefiled matrimonial bed, for most couples, is a prerequisite for destiny fulfillment. However, marriage is not compulsory for those "*who have made themselves eunuchs for the kingdom of heaven's sake*" (Mt 19:12).

Sex is to the Christian married couple what Holy Communion is between Jesus Christ and His Church. As often as husband and wife engage in sexual intimacy, they remind themselves of their vows of oneness. Just as the Blood of Jesus cleanses the body of participants in the ordinance even so sex is the home therapy for a Christian couple. Venereal diseases are demons.

A husband and wife faithful to each other cannot attract sexually-transmitted demons into their lives. For more on this topic get a copy of **MARRIAGE: An Exposition On Christian Marital Relationship** – in the **THE MARANATHA PROJECT** series.

TRAGEDY OF UNBIBLICAL SEXUAL INTIMACY

The tragedy of entrance of sin in the human situation is traceable to the failure or unwillingness of Adam to consummate his marriage to Eve which God initiated in the Garden of Eden when he was a son of God. Satan exploited that lapse and has turned around to use sexual immorality to put the world into bondage. Satan is using perverted sexual relationship to cage married couples in order to render them unfit for God's purpose. If Adam had not fallen, there would have been no sin, sickness or death. Everyone born into this world would have been holy unto the Lord. The earth would have been replenished. There would have been no need for God to incarnate as a Man to come into the world to save sinners.

The problems of mankind are traceable to unbiblical use of sexuality in practically every aspect of human activity. The drive for power and money is essentially to gratify sexual appetite in its lurid forms.

Sexual immorality is at the root of everything that has happened, is happening or will happen on earth that is opposed to the plan and purpose of God. The problems of the world are directly proportional to unbiblical use of sexuality in practically every aspect of human activity.

There are not many sinful behavioral acts that are not linked directly or indirectly to the 'door' of women, a reference to unscriptural coition. The three big worldly motivators are power, money and sex. The major motive for seeking power is to have limitless supply of money which is the assured way to have unbridled pleasure of which sexual gratification is the most important aspect. King Solomon tried it and was disappointed. His warning concerning seduction:

> Prov 5:3, 5, 8; 7:26-27
> **For the lips of an immoral woman drip honey, and her mouth is smoother than oil; remove your way far from her, and do not go near the door of her house. For she has cast down many wounded, and all who were slain by her were strong men. Her house is the way to hell, descending to the chambers of death.**

Entanglement with the "door" of a woman is the easiest way of landing in the lake of fire. Preoccupation with sex outside biblical marriage is the propelling force that goads Christians into perdition. "*Stolen water is sweet, and bread eaten in secret is pleasant. But he does not know that the dead are there, that her guests are in the depths of hell*" (Prov 9:17-18).

A believer who in action and thought has subdued the hi-tech sex promo currently pervading the whole world through the Internet, TV and pornographic literature has a very good chance of making it to heaven. Unlike in the early church, sexually-immoral people now have a stranglehold on the modern church.

Sex for fun has charted the course of history in the kingdoms of this world. It is the major factor in the interplay of events in this present evil world.

The First Human Marriage

God joined Adam and Eve in marriage. Adam delayed consummation until he fell out of favor with God. When he did the union became ungodly, their first offspring manifested ungodly traits eventually becoming a murderer.

Angels Left Their Estate

Angels transformed themselves into men, married the daughters of men. The union produced a polluted race of giants. God destroyed the then world with a flood of waters.

Confusion At Babel

The motive behind the building of the Tower of Babel was the beginning of idolatry, a religious sacrifice that is always accompanied with sexual immorality.

Corruption In Sodom And Gomorrah

The inhabitants of Sodom and Gomorrah polluted the Promised Land with sexual perversion.

Expulsion From Promised Land

The Jews were expelled from the Promised Land largely due to their lack of discipline in sex-related sins.

1. Abraham and Hagar produced children of the bondwoman, who are infernally opposed to the Jews and Jewish state, a type of the conflict between God and Satan.

2. Reuben and Bilhah deprived the first born of Jacob three blessings: kingship, priesthood and double portion. It became the root of long-drawn household wickedness in the congregation of Israel such as the rebellion of Dathan, Korah and Abihu.

3. Judah's incest with Tamar his daughter-in-law delayed the coming of the Lord for generations.

Sexual immorality can lead to the acquisition of demons and sexually-transmitted diseases, loss of inheritance, diversion of destiny, war, perversion of justice, rejection of the Gospel and eternal death. A single demon can prevent a Christian from participating in the rapture of the Church of Jesus Christ.

A CHRISTIAN'S IDEAL SEX LIFE

Sexual immorality should have no place in the life of a Christian.

> 1 Cor 6:9-10
> **Do you not know that the unrighteous will not inherit the kingdom of God? Do not be deceived. Neither fornicators, nor idolaters, nor adulterers, nor homosexuals, nor sodomites ... will inherit the kingdom of God"**

Christians are the constituent parts of the Body of Christ and also members of each other within the Family of God. *"So we, being many, are one body in Christ, and individually members of one another"* (Rom 12:5). At the point of regeneration every believer is sealed into the Body of Christ: every born again Christian occupies a specific space in the mystical body of Christ described by Apostle Paul variously to be like a human body, a building or an army. Engrafting into the Body of Christ is done supernaturally by the Holy Spirit. As for fitting location into the Body of Christ of any particular saint "*God has set the members, each one of them, in the body just as He pleased*" (1 Cor 12:18). Whatever a member does, good or bad, affects other members inter se and the mystical Body of Christ as a whole.

Christ and His church are one. Husband and wife are one. The wife must submit to her husband else she would be headless. A married man must love his wife because she is his body; he is her head. Christ loved His body and gave Himself for her. Husbands are enjoined to love their wives even to death. Married couples should not see themselves as separate individuals; they are one, but occupying two spots in the mystical Body of Christ.

A married woman is not doing her husband any favor by satiating him with her sexual ministration. It is her divine duty. Likewise is the husband. This is the meaning of 1 Cor 7:4. God will hold the guilty partner responsible for destiny diversion resulting from misuse of coition or the lack of it. Sex is marriage and marriage is sex.

In this endtime sex is for destiny fulfillment. If you can forebear, it is better to avoid it. Life is more enjoyable without sex. Paul an unmarried Apostle said: "*I wish that all men were even as I myself*" (1 Cor 7:7). Paul had ample time to concentrate on his divine call. There is more time to focus on things of eternal value and enjoy quality fellowship with the Lord without marriage – 1 Cor 7:32-33.

Suppressing libido like enduring an ungodly marriage is not virtuous. If you cannot forebear marry. It is not a sin to be married. Some mission work requires a 'help meet' to be successful. For others a spouse could be a hindrance to destiny fulfillment.

Discipline is required especially in the area of childbearing. Non-coital sexual indulgence is sin: masturbation, stimulation, sex with artificial organs, sex with animals and same-sex – these are acts of done by whoremongers. Those called by the name of the Lord should not even **think** of being involved with such abominable deeds.

It must be understood that there is no free sex. Sexual immorality is not fun. Playing games with God's creative power invokes divine wrath. The first act of sexual intercourse with a new partner creates an ungodly soul-tie that can if unbroken arm Satan with the legal right to prevent a Christian from entering heaven at the point of death or rapture, whichever occurs first. That is why apart from the desire to live long, misuse of the sex organ is responsible for most cases of perdition.

In this dispensation of grace, the primary purpose of sex is companionship, not childbearing. To marry and have children is not sin. However, it is the undefiled matrimonial bed that is expected to produce the Israeli and Gentile Remnants who will repopulate the earth after the Day of the Lord.

For the avoidance of doubt, there is no free sex. It is either engaged in as an expression of companionship to fulfill divine destiny or frivolously with serious eternal consequence.

... in the Scroll of the Book it is written ...

on **POWER**

"Nevertheless do not rejoice in this, that the spirits are subject to you, but rather rejoice because your names are written in heaven." (Lk 10:20)

But Jesus said to him, "Put your sword in its place, for all who take the sword will perish by the sword." (Mt 26:52)

Let this mind be in you which was also in Christ Jesus, who being in the form of God ... made Himself of no reputation, and ... being found in appearance as a man, He humbled Himself and became obedient to the point of death, even the death of the cross. (Phil 2:5-8)

Part Four

POWER

8

POWER AND CORRUPTION

God has spoken once,
Twice I have heard this:
That power belongs to God.
And Jesus came and spoke to them,
saying, "All authority has been given
to Me in heaven and on earth.
Ps 62:11; Mt 28:18

STATEMENTS ON POWER

"Power tends to corrupt, and absolute power corrupts absolutely." Lord Acton

"Power corrupts, but lack of power corrupts absolutely." Adlai Stevenson

"Unlimited power is apt to corrupt the minds of those who possess it." William Pitt the Elder

"The most awful thing about power is not that it corrupts absolutely but that it makes people so utterly boring, so predictable..." Chinua Achebe

"All Hollywood corrupts; absolute Hollywood corrupts absolutely." Edmund Wilson

(source: Microsoft ® Encarta ® 2009. © 1993-2008)

From the above quotations it has been posited that absolute power corrupts absolutely, lack of power corrupts absolutely, being rich and famous can corrupt absolutely, and unlimited power corrupts the mind to some degree, maybe not absolutely: corruptive pattern is hopelessly discernible. Before considering the corrupting power of POWER or the lack of it, let us define power.

WHAT IS POWER?

Power is the possession of the capacity, strength and ability to do something. The creative power of God has the capacity of bringing into physical manifestation things that were not previously in existence. Power is the ability to control creation and the aura to be respected, honored and feared. It is the ability to have one's way in all circumstances; one to be looked up to and a dispenser of beneficence.

Of the two realms in the universe the spiritual is superior to and controls the physical domain. There are four kinds of spirit in the universe.

1. God, The Almighty. God is SPIRIT.

2. Holy angels. Angles in God's service are spirits.

3. Fallen spirit beings. Evil spirits, fallen angels and demons are spirits.

4. Human beings. Man is a spirit.

Some of the attributes of God include omnipotence, omnipresence, omniscience and immutability. His Almightiness means He is Adonai the Strong and Most powerful One, Creator of all things visible and invisible. God is the head of all principalities and powers; He is the source of all power. All power in the visible and invisible realms originated in Him.

In the beginning of creation, God expanded His invisible Kingdom by creating the material universe for His children and specifically gave the earth to the sons of men for an inheritance. At that time there was one God, one kingdom and one will. Lucifer's rebellion created a chasm between the heavens and the earth and paved the way for the temptation and fall of Adam that brought two kingdoms, two wills, and corruption thereby making Satan the god of this world.

CORRUPTION OF GOD'S POWER

Lucifer corrupted the power of God delegated to him and a third of the angelic host to rule the earth prior to the creation of man. In his rebellion Lucifer and his cohorts attempted to use their 'power' to dethrone God. See Isa 14:12-14. This corrupt power entered the world through the transgression of Adam and Eve.

WHAT IS CORRUPTION?

To be corrupt is to be depraved, perverted, influenced by bribery and perverted from fidelity. Corruption entered the world through Adam's transgression. When Adam fell, corruption, sorrow and death came into the world. All sinned and came short of the glory of God. Corruption of the human species led to the judgment of the flood, but God saved Noah and his family of seven. The postdiluvian reintroduced corruption into the world through the spirit of Jezebel at the Tower of Babel. That is why there is corruption all over the world, and it has been growing in strength since then.

The love of money, inordinate quest for power and sexual indulgence outside marriage are some of the fruits of corruption. The Western world has over the years used welfarism to stem the most brazen effects of corruption, unlike what is happening in the Less Developing Countries especially in the African continent.

Corruption in general terms is moral deterioration and depravity. An instance of this is exemplified by the perversion of a person's integrity in the performance of official or public duty or work by demanding financial inducement or undue favor. Therefore, a corrupt person is dishonest, bribable, crooked, fraudulent, dishonorable, unscrupulous and untrustworthy. A corrupt society or institution is rotten, polluted, putrid, decayed, putrescent, tainted, infected and contaminated. Bribery which is an inducement to act dishonestly or unfaithfully is an integral part of corruption.

THE SPIRIT BEHIND

There is a spirit behind every activity in the world. The two spirits at work in the world today are the Holy Spirit manifesting through those who have received Him. "*Now we have received, not the spirit of the world, but the spirit which is of God; that we might know the things that are freely given to us of God"* (1 Cor 2:12). This is the spirit of truth that governs the lives of those who are not of this world. There is another spirit that manifests human depravity. It is the spirit of the world. Those who operate with this spirit are of the world. The Holy Spirit is a person. So also is Satan who is the spirit of the world. He is the prince of the power of the air, energizing and controlling the children of disobedience. Every human activity on earth promotes either God or Satan. Human interaction is centered on self, the god of this world.

The spirit of Babylon originated in Satan and manifested initially with Eve in the Garden of Eden. After the Flood of Noah, it dominated the relationship between Semiramis and Nimrod her son-husband. This is the spirit that can manipulate a man to be father-grandfather, mother-wife, brother-husband or sister-wife of a person. It causes people to be born with bastard spirits, wrong pairing of blood relatives in marriage and spiritual marriages of intractable dimensions. It is responsible for human disasters.

Nimrod was a Cushite, a great hunter who ruled Babylon as a dictator for 185 years. It was during his time that the Tower of Babel, the symbol of idolatry, was built. Nimrod and Semiramis taught the black race and the rest of the world how to worship the devil, heavenly bodies, sun, moon, stars and sex organs. Long after Nimrod was assassinated, Semiramis gave birth to Tammuz. She claimed Nimrod impregnated her from heaven; hence her title of 'Queen of heaven.' The spirit that worked in her exploded wickedness in and through Queen Jezebel. She committed many atrocious sins against God and those who were followers of the God of Israel. She converted her husband into a terrible wizard. Her children followed after her.

The spirit of Jezebel is antichristian, supervises Satan's ministry of stealing, killing and destroying God's people and His plans. It delights in the prophets of Baal who function in the office of false prophets with counterfeit power. The spirit of Jezebel is vengeful, unforgiving and idolatrous exhibiting traits of pride arrogance and haughtiness. These Babylonian spirits control international trade, fashion, organize international fashion shows merchandising all kinds of seductive dresses, cosmetics and make-up, cause looseness in life resulting in all kinds of sexual perversion. They induce people to make human sacrifice to Satan through abortion, murder by witchcraft often truncating destinies through polygamy, alcoholism and drug abuse.

The gospel of Christ is the power of God for salvation. But men prefer to seek esoteric power in opposition to God. Men know God but refuse to acknowledge Him as the Creator and source of all life; hence they worship, serve and seek after creation rather than the Creator. Everyone born into this world has an inbuilt mechanism for knowing God and the freewill to choose whether to service Him or not. There is no excuse for idolatry. It is always a deliberate choice to worship, serve and obey creation rather than the Creator.

Men seek satanic power to be independent of God. Men seek satanic power to control creation for evil purposes – wickedness. The heart of unregenerate mankind is the manufacturer of wickedness. See Ezekiel 17:9. Wickedness is something that is 'bad, mischievous, injurious, hurtful i.e. giving pain or causing unhappiness.' (AMG Reference Bible). It is the hideous thing, a calamity or tragedy that is fashioned against someone. A wicked person derives joy from his wicked deeds. The purpose of Satan ultimately is to convert man to his beastly depraved nature.

The world was created perfect but through one man's sin corruption, sorrow and death came into the world. The gospel of Christ is the power of God for salvation in all its ramifications. But corruption is the gospel of opposition to God and His righteousness. It is a virus that has the capacity to putrefy anyone or anything it touches. It is a curse, and sin against God, fellowmen and self. It is the foundation for wickedness, poverty of the spirit and backwardness – the iniquity that has tainted human interaction. Corruption is to the kingdom of darkness what anointing is to the kingdom of Light. By reason of anointing yokes are broken, burdens lifted, vessels empowered for service. The oil that lubricates activities in God's kingdom is the anointing. The power that drives activities in the dark kingdoms of this world is rooted in corruption.

Nothing tainted with corruption can ever stand before God because His eyes are too pure and holy to behold iniquity. As a pollutant corruption affects man and nature negatively. Esoteric power is the harbinger of corruption and money is its currency.

Satan blinds the eyes of men through bewitchment. Satanic power has present, earthly but ephemeral reward. The quest for power is the root of corruption, epitomized by:

1. Pride.

2. Desire to be like the Most High. This is occultism.

3. Making a name for self, as happened at Babel.

4. Desire for other things – unnatural things. Changing the natural for the esoteric.

5. Dissatisfaction with natural things. Homosexual and lesbian tendencies.

6. Propagation of wrong doctrine, which is another gospel.

Power brings money and money gives access to good and bad things of life. How a person acquires power depends on the spirit controlling his or her life. How a person spends money depends on his or her purpose in life. Some people are living for now without eternity in view. They are beasts of the earth.

In most parts of the world, especially developing countries, governmental power is the license for poverty alleviation. Hence men and women do unimaginable things to gain political power to become rich. Power and corruption are two sides of the same coin.

Corruption has many ramifications; preaching the gospel for filthy lucre is part of it. The two areas Satan fights men and women of God hardest are *power* and *sex*. Both are *money*-driven. Power gives access to money and pleasure. Money confers power on the holder for acquiring more of it. Power is connected with pride, glory and self-actualization. Sexual immorality has many ramifications. It takes the grace of God for a child of God who has accumulated stupendous wealth not to be ruled by money. It takes the special grace of God for a child of God of great means not to be involved in sexual immorality, especially of the non-coital nature.

BEWITCHMENT

Corruption works with bewitchment. To bewitch is to cast a spell on a person, an animal or an inanimate object. Bewitchment is an evil influence exerted through spells, jinxes, enchantments, divinations and incantations with a view to steal, kill or destroy people, families and nations. The bewitching medium is a charm usually an object into which demons have been programmed to carry out wicked acts. The purpose of charms is to enslave and mislead through demonic influences.

The energy of witchcraft is bewitchment. Witchcraft is an evil force operating in darkness with the purpose of changing things from their original state. Witches and familiar spirits work hand in hand their primary function being to bend what is straight and make it crooked, alter divine purpose to conform to their wicked intentions of destroying God's creation.

Satanic agents use witchcraft spirits to bewitch people in order to control, intimidate and manipulate them at their will. Those who bewitch people in this way are called witches and wizards – for females and males respectively. Witches and wizards are the epitome of wickedness.

Christ has restored the original power of God to those who follow Him. Jesus died on the cross to remove the divine curse on man and creation. Gal 3:13. He shed His blood in seven ways not only for the remission of human sin but to remove the corruption Adamic sin brought into the human situation.

Jesus shed his blood in several ways to redeem fallen mankind and died on the cross to remove the curse placed on man and creation consequent upon Adam's transgression. By paying the penalty for sin and the attendant curse, Jesus has been invested with all power. He declared: "*All authority has been given to Me in heaven and on earth*" (Mt 28:18). This power is now available to those called by His name to dominate the earth until His second coming to restitute all things.

Unfortunately, unrighteous mammon, which is the god of riches, has successfully invaded the church of Jesus Christ in this endtime. It would appear the days when children of God coveted after spiritual gifts are over. Now it is mammon with ecclesiastical sanction.

Mammon is the epitome of dark powers. Unbelievers are darkness. Believers through sinful conduct can be in darkness. The energy of corruption is idolatry. Idolatry is worship of anyone or anything other than Almighty God.

COVETOUSNESS

In the past things coveted were usually superior to present possession.

1. Lucifer coveted God's throne and wanted to be like the Most High.

2. The angels that fell coveted the power of being independent to being holy servants of God and His children.

3. Some angels coveted humans by leaving their own estate to mingle with daughters of men.

4. Men are leaving the natural use of the woman to marry same-sex.

5. Humans covet having sex with beasts abhorring God's beautiful gift of heterosexual conjugation.

Money is power; it gives access to the good as well as bad things of life. In a bid to have money and be powerful, men and women sell their souls to the god of money. Men sear their conscience for money; women ridicule their bodies for money. 'There is no brother in business' means money is more important than blood ties in family and marriage. When money is flowing freely hatred and rejection are abetted. Hence 'no money, no friend' is real in many life situations.

The only way to solve the problem of corrupt accumulation of money and material things in a country, organization or family is to make it unprofitable. And the only way to make it unprofitable is to insist on restitution without time limitation.

Corruption in the world was created by lust. Lust is intensive desire to gain satisfaction through sight "seeing what is good to see", the cravings of the flesh and to prove that one has arrived and worthy of reckoning with, which is social esteem according to Abraham Maslow. Power without control breeds anarchy.

9

DANGERS OF PURSUING MONEY SEX AND POWER

*"For what will it profit a man if he gains
the whole world, and loses his own soul?
Or what will a man give in exchange
for his soul?"*
Mk 8:36-37

CARES OF THIS LIFE

Sin is attractive. Riches are desirable. However, unbridled desire for wealth of this world is the building block for an evil heart of unbelief. Heb 3:12-14. Satan, the god of this evil world delights in blinding the minds of sinners from receiving the gospel of God's abundant grace. *"Now these are the ones sown among thorns; they are the ones who hear the word, and the cares of this world, the deceitfulness of riches, and the desires for other things entering in choke the word, and it becomes unfruitful"* (Mk 4:18-19).

Riches are not evil but they have the capacity to deceive the holder. In the fight of faith, two phenomena that challenge belief are persecution and material prosperity. Persecution is external, visible and can be checkmated by corporate prayer and resistance. Material wellbeing is internal, insidious and resides in the heart that is prone to wickedness. "*The heart is deceitful above all things, and desperately wicked; who can know it?*" (Jer 17:9). Those who trust in riches cannot be saved.

The problems that rich people encounter are usually two-fold:

1. Inordinate attention to the things of this world expressed exclusively in political, social, economic, educational or sporting endeavor that has nothing to do with one's divine destiny thereby neglecting the one thing that is needful in every life.

2. Deceitfulness of riches, expressed in acquiring immense wealth for self-fulfillment, as opposed to having and controlling wealth for a good cause – the mandate of Jesus.

Putting confidence in the security of material wealth and having hope in the capacity of riches to solve future expectations are attempts to substitute self for God. It is difficult for a heart in want of nothing to be fully focused on God and things of eternal value. '*Give us day by day our daily bread'* means there is a void in our life that only God can fill. Where that gap is imagined to be non-existent, God becomes distant and irrelevant in daily pursuit. The prayer of Jabez was prompted by things that were needful in his life.

Everybody has an unmet need. A rich young man inquired from Jesus what he needed to do to inherit eternal life.

> Mt 22:21-26
> **Jesus said to him, "If you want to be perfect, go, sell what you have and give to the poor, and you will have treasure in heaven; and come, follow Me." But when the young man heard that saying, he went away sorrowful, for he had great possessions. Then Jesus said to His disciples, "Assuredly, I say to you that it is hard for a rich man to enter the kingdom of heaven. And again I say to you, it is easier for a camel to go through the eye of a needle than for a rich man to enter the kingdom of God." When His disciples heard it, they were greatly astonished, saying, "Who then can be saved?" But Jesus looked at them and said to them, "With men this is impossible, but with God all things are possible."**

Another *"certain rich man who was clothed in purple and fine linen and fared sumptuously every day"* died and landed in hellfire. Although he regretted his earthly lifestyle, he discovered it was too late to make amends. Over-indulgence in earthly pleasure is guaranteed to harden the heart, which erodes saving faith. Although it is hard *"for a rich man to enter the kingdom of God,"* it is even harder for a chronically poor person to make it to heaven. Just as riches foster love of the world, all-round lack is also a harbinger of worldliness. Therefore, it is wise to use material things of this world without abusing or snubbing them in destiny pursuit.

MYSTERY OF INIQUITY

The mystery of iniquity is that Satan works to convert every unsaved human being on earth into his sunken nature. Even as the Hypostatic Chip empowered by the Holy Spirit is converting every believer into Christ-likeness, even so the principality in charge of unsaved people is strenuously making mankind to manifest the traits of Satanism to a beastly level. What is preventing full manifestation of humans as beasts is the presence of the Holy Spirit and the church in the world. In the second half of the tribulation period, the 'seed' of Satan will develop fully as beasts on the earth. *"Now the Spirit expressly says that in latter times some will depart from the faith, giving heed to deceiving spirits and doctrines of demons, speaking lies in hypocrisy, having their own conscience seared with a hot iron, forbidding to marry, and commanding to abstain from foods which God created to be received with thanksgiving by those who believe and know the truth"* (1 Tim 4:1-3).

There is worldwide undue excitement in the occult together with amusement in sports, music, entertainment and visual pleasure. At the personal level the goal is self-actualization, satisfaction of sensual pleasure unrestrained by the laws of Almighty God. Morality has become primitive. Modernism means unbridled lust of the eyes, lust of the flesh and pride of life, penchant for exotic foods not for healthy living but to gratify the belly, a life of ease, and over-indulgence in sleep and pleasure. Others include preferment for public approbation and the praise of men, power of control over other people and pre-occupation with self.

This is the end time and the platform for endtime sins has already been laid. *"But know this, that in the last days perilous times will come: For men will be lovers of themselves, lovers of money, boasters, proud, blasphemers, disobedient to parents, unthankful, unholy, unloving, unforgiving, slanderers, without self-control, brutal, despisers of good, traitors, headstrong, haughty, lovers of pleasure rather than lovers of God, having a form of godliness but denying its power"* (2 Tim 3:1-5). Backsliding or falling away from the faith delivered to us, giving heed to seducing spirits and giving heed to doctrines of devils, speaking lies in hypocrisy that can sear the conscience as a hot iron are some of the precursors of tribulation period sins. They have begun to gain world-wide attraction – Rev 9:20-21.

1. Occultism: demon worship; there is witchcraft in the church in this Laodicea-church era.

2. Murder mostly using remote control through witchcraft. The use of poisoned food in the public domain is part of chemical warfare.

3. Abortions, with state sponsorship. Terrorism and gangsterism. Armed conflicts.

4. Sorceries manifesting as drug abuse. The use drug is designed to gain control of the human will and convert to beastly nature.

5. Fornication in its lurid forms: sexual perversion – homosexuality, lesbianism and bestiality. Sodomy. Adultery and fornication between humans as deviant behavior is no longer attracting public attention; it has become accepted as the normal way of life.

6. Stealing. Corruption. Pen and armed robbery.

BIBLICAL EXAMPLES OF PURSUING MONEY, SEX AND POWER

The pursuit of wealth for personal gain is a harbinger of eternal death. In the following biblical examples, the transgressors reaped a huge harvest of woe and doom.

Achan. *Lust for Money and riches* - Joshua 7.

Achan stole the accursed thing from Jericho in defiance of the commandment of God: (Josh 7:21). He wanted to be rich and famous. He brought untimely death to his nuclear family including livestock. (Josh 7:24-25).

Gainsaying Of Korah, Abiram And Dathan. *Tussle for Power.* Num 16

These men rebelled against the leadership of Moses and Aaron. Korah a Levite was aggrieved for being bypassed in the appointment of head of the Kohathites. Abiram and Dathan were frustrated for missing out on the kingship and priesthood of Israel through their father Reuben's indiscretion in sleeping with Bilhah, his father's concubine. Together they mobilized the support of 250 princes of Israel. The Lord intervened in the matter and gave instant judgment: Num 16:23-33. Korah, Dathan and Abiram their wives and sons who joined the rebellion went down into hellfire without dying – the first in history. Also the 250 princes were devoured by fire from the Lord as they were offering incense at the Altar.

Leprosy Of Gehazi. *Covetousness for Money and Personal Property.*

Gehazi went behind his master to collect money and materials Elisha rejected from Naaman as reward for healing him of leprosy. The leprosy of Naaman clung on him and his posterity forever.

Profanity Of Esau. *Disdain for Birthright.*

Esau sold his birthright to Jacob for a plate of pottage. The profanity of Esau stems from the fact that he was a man of the flesh with no regard for the things of the spirit. He despised his birthright. When he wanted to inherit the promises God made to his father and grandfather, he was rejected. He realized his mistake and wept, but it was too late. As Christians our heritage in Christ Jesus are immeasurably weighty and non-perishable. (2 Cor 2:8) To despise Christian heritage is the greatest tragedy that can befall a child of God.

Fornication Of Reuben. *Sexual Pleasure.*

Reuben enjoyed a few minutes' sexual pleasure with Bilhah his father's fourth wife and was disinherited of three things: the kingship, the priesthood and a double portion of his father's wealth. His progeny suffered premature death, high casualty rate in wars and frustration such as Korah's rebellion.

Error Of Balaam. *Money and Recognition.* Num 22: 1-41

The Doctrine of Balaam: Love of money, disobeying God, selfish ambition and divining for money. Others are interfering with God's kingdom purposes, using spiritual gifts to oppose God and putting stumbling blocks in the way of God's people. He taught the doctrine of the Nicolaitans. He was killed when Israel invaded Moab.

Covetousness Of Judas Iscariot – *Power and Ecclesiastical Influence.*

Judas betrayed his master Jesus for thirty pieces of silver. He lost his bishopric and apostleship and ended up hanging himself.

Corruption Of Governor Felix – *Money*

In the ministry of Apostle Paul, Governor Felix was convicted of sin but vacillated from believing in Christ. He wanted Paul to give him money rather than show him the way of salvation. Acts 24:24-25

Self-Exaltation Of King Herod – *Pride*

He was eaten by worms (Acts 12:23).

Procrastination Of King Agrippa – *Sensual Pleasure*

Acts 26:28 "*Then Agrippa said to Paul, You almost persuade me to become a Christian.*"

Infidelity Of Hymenaeus And Alexander - "*... of whom I delivered to Satan that they may learn not to blaspheme*" (1 Tim 1:20).

Backsliding Of Demas - 2 Tim 4:10

Samson's Delusions – *Presumptuous Faith*

Samson deluded himself by thinking that the grace of God would always work in his life regardless of his present action. The devil deceived Samson to believe that he was invincible and untouchable. When the Lord comes, He comes with an entourage of signs and miracles. The gifts and calling are irrevocable but when the Lord Himself departs from a person, that person is left without any protection and falls into the snare of the devil. It is a tragedy to die prematurely, destiny unfulfilled and with one's enemies like Samson.

The Vainglory Of Ananias And Saphira – Acts 5:1

Ananias and Saphira lied to the Holy Ghost and died at the feet of Apostle Peter. They wanted the applause of men. In today's church, 'white' official and diplomatic lies are no longer regarded as sin. All liars and those that love and make lies shall not inherit the kingdom of God.

Strange Fire Of Nadab And Abihu Lev 10:1

The first and second sons of Aaron through pride and self-exaltation and in a drunken state offered strange fire at the altar and died before the Lord. God did not send them. In this endtime church strange fires are being offered all over the place in the name of worshipping God partly because instant judgment does not take place as in the case of Nadab and Abihu. But the day of reckoning will surely come.

David's Adultery

David's adultery with Beersheba resulted in murder to cover it up. His problem began when he found himself in the wrong place at the wrong time. At a time when kings went to war David was relaxing at home. The enemy struck and caused him great distress. Usually the sin of adultery leads to other heinous sins. Though he repented, prayed, fasted and was forgiven, the "sword did not depart from his house."

1) The child resulting from the adultery died.

2) Amnon David's heir apparent committed incest with Tamar his half-sister and was murdered by Absalom.

3) Absalom attempted to overthrow his father King David and slept with his father's ten concubines "in the sight of all Israel."

4) David become a fugitive and ran from place to place.

5) Solomon who succeeded David as king married 700 wives plus 300 concubines. Consequently, he went into idolatry by worshipping the gods of his foreign wives, disobeying God's warning.

It is a tragedy to think that unscriptural pleasure is cheap. David used his presidential fiat to deploy Bathsheba on his royal bed. The price he paid was almost unbearable. To allow five minutes of sensual pleasure to deprive a person of his or her heritage is a tragedy.

FOCUS ON DESTINY

The one thing that is needful is to focus on fulfilling one's destiny regardless of the circumstance. History is replete with people with physical challenges who excelled in their chosen areas of endeavor and fulfilled their God-given destinies. To be without abundant material resources is not a tragedy. To be unpopular, uncelebrated in this life without earthly accolades is not a tragedy. It is a tragedy to be born in sin, live and die in sin without accepting Christ's offer of salvation.

If you are an unbeliever you have no excuse for refusing Christ's free offer of salvation of your soul. He has paid the price. All you are required to do is accept His substitutional death on the cross by calling on Him to be your Lord and personal Savior.

If you are a Christian you have absolutely no excuse for missing the rapture of the Church. Those who are seeking the glory that belongs exclusively to God, coveting what belongs to others through worldliness and fleshly immorality and the love of unrighteous mammon are likely to miss the rapture and face the wrath of the antichrist.

There are many tragic situations in contemporary society which are unavoidable, for example physical death. However, the tragedy of landing in hellfire is avoidable.

Hypostatic Union Is Success

When God looks down on earth from heaven He sees 'gods' that resemble Him in earthen vessels. Originating from His heart as the Incorruptible Seed, these "gods" transform willing mankind to imitate and be like Christ. *"Jesus answered them, 'Is it not written in your law, "I said, 'You are gods'"? If He called them gods, to whom the word of God came (and the Scripture cannot be broken), do you say of Him whom the Father sanctified and sent into the world, 'You are blaspheming,' because I said, 'I am the Son of God'"?*

Part Five

SUCCESS IN LIFE

10

THE INCORRUPTIBLE SEED

*Since you have purified your souls in obeying
the truth through the Spirit in sincere love of the brethren,
love one another fervently with a pure heart, having been born
again, not of corruptible seed but incorruptible, through the
word of God which lives and abides forever.*
1 Pet 1:22-23

GOD HAS A FAMILY

In the beginnings of Scripture God by the hand of His Son Jesus Christ created the visible universe for the purpose of expanding the family and kingdom of God. The heaven of heavens became God's throne but the earth He gave to mankind whom He created in His image and likeness. Everything created by God was perfect. God made Adam governor of the earth. Adam needed a test to become a god forever. He failed.

HYPOSTATIC UNION

Adam was created in the image and likeness of God. The image of God in Adam was the breath of life, which goes by different names in the bible: incorruptible see, His spirit, son of God. I call it 'Hypostatic Chip' because of its activities that resemble a computer chip with different kinds of programs but nonfunctional except inserted into a computer system and activated by the user.

When Adam and Eve sinned, the image of God or Hypostatic Chip in their spirit that made them sons of God was withdrawn back to heaven where it came from. They 'died' as God said with immediate separation from God and gradual degradation of the body to physical death and eternal separation from God in that state. In mercy God provided a way of escape from eternal death.

The transgression of Adam and Eve in Genesis chapter three interrupted but did not abrogate the original plan of God for man on earth. The offspring of Adam and Eve in their fallen state manifested the characteristics of Satan their new father such as unbelief, disobedience and wickedness. All that come into this world do so from 'beneath' a reference to hell, having inherited Adam's sin, and born in iniquity. All are susceptible to death – spiritual, physical and eternal death, which is irreversible separation from God.

REDEMPTION FROM ADAM'S TRANGRESSION

Jesus, the Son of God, has paid the price for Adamic sin, hence reconciling man with God. Those who accept the substitutional sacrifice of Himself on the cross of Calvary can be redeemed and pulled out of the fires of hell to inherit eternal life.

Jesus came into the world to fulfill what was programmed in His Chip. He followed the program faithfully even when it was painful to His flesh and soul. Jesus came into the world to:

1. Pay the price for the redemption of what God lost – human and material.

2. Re-unite earth with heaven with a sacrifice on Calvary's Cross.

3. Build a replacement for the fallen angels, namely the Church from believing Jews and Gentiles.

4. Remove the curse placed on earth for the sake of Adam.

5. Revert to position before the transgression of Adam.

6. Make restitution of all things by replenishing the earth with godly natural human beings.

7. Surrender kingdom to God the Father. Handing over the visible kingdom to God the Father will bring the saying '*Your kingdom come, Your will be done on earth as it is in heaven*' to pass so that the Father will resume His position as "all in all" eternally.

Jesus paid the price of redemption when He offered His life a ransom by dying the death of the cross. He shed His blood in seven ways to provide total redemption for human spirit, soul and body. Jesus rose from the dead, ascended into heaven and is seated at the right hand of God waiting for His Body to be completely built and united with Him at the rapture of the church.

CHOSEN, PECULIAR, KINGDOM OF PRIESTS

On the Day of Pentecost, about two thousand years ago, the Holy Spirit came into the world to plant Hypostatic Chips into willing vessels. Since then to this day, the job of the Holy Spirit in the world has been to show fallen mankind how to regain the lost Incorruptible Seed which is eternal life. It begins with the hearing of faith, conviction of sin that brings the new birth to those who exercise their free-will in reverse order to what Adam did. Adam used freewill in his soul to reject God, inviting Satan into his spirit, which was in his blood. The same free-will, which is the likeness of God in man, must be used to reject Satan and accept God in human flesh, the Lord Jesus Christ, who paid the price of redemption with the life in His untainted blood.

HYPOSTATIC CHIPS

The life and ministry of Jesus, the last Adam, demonstrate in a perfect way the design to fuse 'gods' with earthen vessels in a hypostatic union. Unless a person consciously rejects the inherited image of Satan in order to receive the image of God that person cannot begin to see, understand or appreciate the things of God. The person is still living in Adam's original sin that confers eternal death.

Therefore, fallen mankind is in dire need of the Incorruptible Seed which is obtainable through genuine repentance. To repent and be born again therefore is to reject the image of Satan, a demon and accept the image of Jesus, a Hypostatic Chip, which confers sonship of God. For those already in the Lord what they need is growth in grace attainable through renewing the mind with the word of God in order to be perfect in spirit, soul and body.

TELEPHONE HANDSET ANALOGY

Although all have sinned and come short of the glory of God deserving banishment in the lake of fire, God has reserved the final judgment for Jesus Christ at various times in the future. Meanwhile, Jesus is taking out a people for Himself from believing Jews and Gentiles. When that sub-program is completed presently, the current dispensation will come to an end transiting into the next and last human dispensation – the kingdom of God on earth.

All those who participate in the four future raptures of the Tribulation Period which is fast approaching will be the Kingdom of Priests that will rule the earth with Jesus forever. (1 Pet 2:9). At the second coming of Christ a 'Remnant' of righteous natural people will be selected to multiply and replenish the earth as decreed by God in Gen 1:28. That means there will be a reversion to God's original plan that was interrupted by the transgression of Adam and pollution of the earth with sin.

Therefore, knowledge of the plan of God and what the Holy Spirit is saying to the church NOW is important to avoid the deceitfulness of sin engineered by the natural desire for money, sex and power. That is the foundation of good success, which is what really matters from heaven's perspective.

11

IMITATING CHRIST

*Imitate me, just as I also imitate Christ. Looking
unto Jesus, the author and finisher of our faith,
who for the joy that was set before Him endured
the cross, despising the shame, and has sat down
at the right hand of the throne of God.*
1 Cor 11:1; Heb 12:2

HOW TO IMITATE JESUS

To **imitate Jesus** is to follow His footsteps. To **follow Him** means to be like Him. To **be like Jesus** means to have biblical answers to **five cardinal questions** of life. To have correct answers to the cardinal questions of life means to have the **attributes of a child of God**. "*But each one in his own order: Christ the firstfruits, afterward those who are Christ's at His coming*" (1 Cor 15:23). Jesus is the "*firstfruits*" and all who desire to imitate him must be like Him.

In 1 Cor 11:1 Apostle Paul said "*Imitate me as I imitate Christ.*" How did Apostle Paul imitate Christ? Saul was a blasphemer, wasted the church of Jesus Christ and "*persecuted this Way to the death, binding and delivering into prisons both men and women. For you have heard of my former conduct in Judaism, how I persecuted the church of God beyond measure and tried to destroy it. And I punished them often in every synagogue and compelled them to blaspheme; and being exceedingly enraged against them, I persecuted them even to foreign cities*" (Acts 22:4; Gal 1:13 Acts 26:11).

On Damascus road the persecutor encountered the power of the Holy Spirit. "*So he, trembling and astonished, said, 'Lord, what do You want me to do?'*" *Then the Lord said to him, "Arise and go into the city, and you will be told what you must do."* Thenceforth, Paul was not disobedient to the heavenly calling and followed Christ to the end.

Everybody on planet earth has a reason for being born. Everybody has a divine destiny. It is rooted in the mandate of Jesus. The earth was created by Jesus Christ for His pleasure and everybody has the opportunity of being part of His kingdom as opposed to being in the kingdom of this present evil world that will soon come to an end. To imitate Jesus therefore is to key into His mandate.

JESUS AND HIS MANDATE

In eternity past, Elohim decided to expand the kingdom of God from the unseen to the visible realm. God the Father gave God the Son a mandate regarding His visible kingdom. The mandate of Jesus has three components in two comings with three finishing points. The first assignment was His incarnation: assuming a human body in order to pay the price of redemption and save what God lost through the rebellion of Lucifer and transgression of Adam and Eve.   Regarding human   redemption, His mandate is to find earthen vessels to put mini-Gods who will have dominion and exercise royal authority over God's visible kingdom with Him. The second assignment in His second coming is to sit on three thrones of glory to judge creation. Thirdly in His second coming, He will re-establish God's literal kingdom with earth dwellers, rule the earth for 1,000 years with a rod of iron in order to restitute all things to conform to the decree of the Godhead and submit the kingdom to the Father to resume His position as Father of all creation.

Of the three finishing points, one is past. On the Cross of Calvary, just before He gave up the ghost, Jesus said: "*It is finished.*" That broke the power of sin and brought redemption to mankind. A few hours to Armageddon, Jesus will say a second "*It is finished.*" That will signal the judgment of the Beast and Gentile nations signaling the beginning of the literal kingdom of God on earth. After the White Throne Judgment, Jesus will submit the Kingdom to the Ancient of Days who will utter the final "*It is finished.*"

The current aspect of His first assignment is to build His church, a replacement for fallen angels "*a chosen generation, a royal priesthood, a holy nation, His own special people, that you may proclaim the praises of Him who called you out of darkness into His marvelous light*" (1 Pet 2:9). Before He ascended into heaven, His parting words were "*As the Father has sent Me, I also send you. Go into all the world and preach the gospel to every creature*" (Jn 20:21; Mk 16:15).

To imitate Jesus means to obey His commandments. You cannot imitate Jesus without following His footsteps and you cannot follow His footsteps without being like Him.

During His earthly ministry, Jesus used the term 'Follow Me' in four senses: He used it to summon men to become His disciples. "*And Jesus, walking by the Sea of Galilee, saw two brothers, Simon called Peter, and Andrew his brother, casting a net into the sea; for they were fishermen. Then He said to them, 'Follow Me, and I will make you fishers of men'*" (Mt 4:18-19). "*The following day Jesus wanted to go to Galilee, and He found Philip and said to him, "Follow Me."* (Jn 1:43). "*As Jesus passed on from there, He saw a man named Matthew sitting at the tax office. And He said to him, "Follow Me." So he arose and followed Him*" (Mt 9:9).

To follow Jesus involves a deliberate decision to be committed to the cause of Christ at all levels of the spiritual ladder. It is facilitated by fire encounter. Baptism by fire means encountering at least one aspect of the attribute of God. Moses encountered fire in the burning bush episode. Isaiah encountered the holiness of God in the year King Uzziah died. Peter and the other Ten encountered His Presence on the shores of the Sea of Tiberias. Paul encountered the fire, voice and thunder of God on Damascus road. In contemporary times many servants of God I know have encountered fires of transformation.

Again, Jesus told His disciples to '*follow Me*' to discourage lukewarnness and double-mindedness in His ministry. "*Then another of His disciples said to Him, 'Lord, let me first go and bury my father' but Jesus said to him, 'Follow Me, and let the dead bury their own dead'*" (Jn 8:21-22). "*Then Jesus said to His disciples, 'If anyone desires to come after Me, let him deny himself, and take up his cross, and follow Me.'*" ... *Jesus said to him, 'If you want to be perfect, go, sell what you have and give to the poor, and you will have treasure in heaven; and come, follow Me'*" (Mt 16:24; Mt 19:21).

Jesus also used the term '*follow Me*' to denote true discipleship as the quality required for making disciples of all nations. More importantly Jesus used the expression to describe what Apostle Paul called tasting the "*powers of the age to come*" in Heb 6:5. It is possible to preach the gospel, make disciples of all nations and miss entry into heaven.

> Jn 13:36; Jn 21:19-22
> **"Simon Peter said to Him, 'Lord, where are You going?' Jesus answered him, 'Where I am going you cannot follow Me now, but you shall follow Me afterward'" (Jn 13:36). "This He spoke, signifying by what death he would glorify God. And when He had spoken this, He said to him, 'Follow Me' (Jn 21:19).**

There is no provision in the New Testament Scripture for Christians to ASK for, desire or do anything that does not fall within the mandate of Jesus. After His glorification Jesus declared "*All authority has been given to Me in heaven and on earth. Go therefore and make disciples of all the nations, baptizing them in the name of the Father and of the Son and of the Holy Spirit, teaching them to observe all things that I have commanded you; and lo, I am with you always, even to the end of the age.*" Amen. That is the mandate Jesus has given to His followers until His return. In the early Church the motive for Christian service was love for the mandate of Christ.

> Acts 2:41, 42, 44, 42; 4:33 (NLT)
> **Those who believed what Peter said were baptized and added to the church—about three thousand in all. They joined with the other believers and devoted themselves to the apostles' teaching and fellowship, sharing in the Lord's Supper and in**

prayer. And all the believers met together constantly and shared everything they had. And the apostles gave powerful witness to the resurrection of the Lord Jesus, and God's great favor was upon them all.

Apostle Paul said:

1 Cor. 4:16 - *Wherefore I beseech you, be ye followers of me* (KJV).

1 Cor. 11:1 - *Be ye followers of me, even as I also am of Christ* (KJV).

Eph 5:1 - *Be ye therefore followers of God, as dear children* (KJV).

1 Thess 1:6 - *And ye became followers of us, and of the Lord, having received the word in much affliction, with joy of the Holy Ghost.* (KJV).

Heb 6:11-12 – *And we desire that each one of you show the same diligence to the full assurance of hope to the end, that you do not become sluggish, but imitate those who through faith and patience inherit the promises.*

BIBLICAL EXAMPLE OF THOSE WHO FOLLOWED GOD

ENOCH

Enoch walked with God; he was righteous and God took him to heaven alive. "*By faith Enoch was taken away so that he did not see death, 'and was not found, because God had taken him'; for before he was taken he had this testimony, that he pleased God'*" (Heb 11:5).

NOAH

Untainted in a world contaminated with offspring from unnatural marriage between fallen spirits and humans, Noah and his family found favor with God. *"By faith Noah, being divinely warned of things not yet seen, moved with godly fear, prepared an ark for the saving of his household, by which he condemned the world and became heir of the righteousness which is according to faith"* (Heb 11:7).

ABRAHAM

The postdiluvian resisted the move of God at the plains of Shinar and became idolaters in the matter of the Tower of Babel. God separated Abraham with promises assuring that in him all the families of the earth shall be blessed. *"By faith Abraham obeyed when he was called to go out to the place which he would receive as an inheritance. And he went out, not knowing where he was going. He waited for the city which has foundations, whose builder and maker is God"* (Heb 11:8, 10). He believed God's promises and it was accounted unto for righteousness. God was so pleased with the faith of Abraham that He called a man of like passion whom He created "a friend."

These Bible characters believed the report that God would send His Son into the world to save them from their sins. We are privileged in this generation to see the fulfillment of that promise. The Son of God has come into the world in human flesh, died on a Roman cross shedding his blood in seven ways to save us from our sins. By dying on the cross He has redeemed us from the curse pronounced by God upon fallen Adam and Eve. As the highest altar on the earth, the cross has re-established the broken link between heaven and earth, making it possible for us to have direct access into the presence of God in heaven.

We are therefore enjoined to look up to Jesus the author and finisher of our faith. Looking up to Jesus has a past, present and future perspective. It means to imitate the lifestyle of Jesus using his earthly life as a pattern of what to do in our own lives. Secondly, it means to follow His instructions and commandments in our present life since obedience is the key for entering into His rest. Thirdly, we are enjoined to believe that His future promises will come to pass: we must be steadfast in our hope and expectation of His return to earth to complete His divine assignment.

12

FIVE CARDINAL QUESTIONS OF LIFE

*And He said to them, "You are from beneath; I am
from above. You are of this world; I am not of this world.
Therefore I said to you that you will die in your sins; for if you
do not believe that I am He, you will die in your sins." Then they
said to Him, "Who are You?" And Jesus said to them, "Just what
I have been saying to you from the beginning.*
Jn 8:23-25

WHO ARE YOU AND WHY ARE YOU HERE?

God is the creator of all things visible and invisible. He created the first man in His image and likeness. Adam was a son of God before his

transgression. Thereafter he became the son of the devil. Descendants of Adam were born in the image of Adam, not

God. Hence all that come into this world do so as children of the devil – "*all have sinned and fall short of the glory of God.*" So, we are all created by God but not everybody is a child of God.

Every activity on earth promotes either the kingdom of God or the kingdom of Satan. We have noted that to look up to Jesus means to follow his footsteps and to follow Jesus means to be like Him. An essential ingredient in striving to be like Jesus is to know who you are.

Some people know they are servants of the devil. Most unbelievers do not know who they are. Adam was created sinless but when he disobeyed God he became a picture of ungodliness. In the Garden of Eden, God looked at Adam and said: 'You are dust.'

Who are unbelievers? Old Testament prophets described them as children of Belial; epitomes of wickedness and ungodliness.

1. John the Baptist described them as brood of vipers.

2. Jesus called them hypocrites, children of the devil.

3. Paul said unbelievers are darkness.

4. Peter described the unrighteous as servants of corruption with eyes full of adultery; dogs.

5. For James sinners are adulterers and adulteresses, enemies of God.

6. John calls them lovers of the world; enemies of God; sinners with the devil.

7. Jude was incisive in his description. In the Epistle he wrote (Jude 8-23, he called unbelievers filthy dreamers, brute beasts, clouds without water, trees

without fruit, twice dead, pulled up by the roots; raging waves of the sea, wandering stars for whom is reserved the blackness of darkness forever; ungodly sinners, grumblers, complainers, lustful, mockers and scoffers, sensual persons, who cause divisions, not having the Spirit but are already in the fires of hell.

FIVE CARDINAL QUESTIONS OF LIFE

Jesus was asked many questions during His earthly ministry such as:

Who are you?
Where did you come from?
Why are you here?
Where are you going from here?
How will you get there?

The difference between the righteous and the unrighteous of this world is that the former have answers to the questions of life. During His earthly walk, Jesus gave answers to these five cardinal questions.

Question #1: ***WHO ARE YOU?***"

In Jn 8:25 the Jews asked Jesus "*Who are You?*" And Jesus said to them, "*Just what I have been saying to you from the beginning.*" At different occasions Jesus responded to the question by saying:

"I am the light of the world."
"I am the door of the sheep."
"I am the bread of life" which came down from heaven.
"I am the good shepherd."
"I who speak to you am He" – the Messiah.
"I am He" – Jesus of Nazareth.

Question #2: ***WHERE DID YOU COME FROM***?

Jn 6:41 "*The Jews then complained about Him, because He said, "I am the bread which came down from heaven.*" In Jn 8:19 Jesus was asked: "*Where is Your Father.*" The Jews wanted to know where He came from. "*And He said to them, 'You are from beneath; I am from above. You are of this world; I am not of this world'*" (Jn 8:23). Jesus came from heaven.

Question #3: ***WHY ARE YOU HERE***?

Jn 6:51 Jesus said: "*I am the living bread which came down from heaven. If anyone eats of this bread, he will live forever; and the bread that I shall give is My flesh, which I shall give for the life of the world.*" On different occasions He said He was here to do His Father's will: to seek and save the lost; to give eternal life to them that believe. "*Most assuredly, I say to you, unless a grain of wheat falls into the ground and dies, it remains alone; but if it dies, it produces much grain. ... for this purpose I came to this hour.* (Jn 12:24, 27).

Question #4: ***WHERE ARE YOU GOING FROM HERE***?

Jesus told the Jews "*I shall be with you a little while longer, and then I go to Him who sent Me.*" (Jn 7:33). He also told His disciples privately He was returning to heaven where He came from. "*What then if you should see the Son of Man ascend where He was before?* (Jn 6:62). Speaking to His Father before going to the cross, Jesus said: "*Now ... I come to You. But now I come to You, and these things I speak in the world, that they may have My joy fulfilled in themselves*" (Jn 17:11, 13).

Question #5: ***HOW WILL YOU GET THERE?***

Jesus said by laying down His life for the brethren. "*Greater love has no one than this, than to lay down one's life for his friends*" (Jn 15:13). For this purpose Jesus came into the world to give His life a ransom for many. "*... If anyone eats of this bread, he will live forever; and the bread that I shall give is My flesh, which I shall give for the life of the world.*"

Born again rapture-ready Christians have answers to the five cardinal questions of life. Old Testament saints knew who they were and what they came to earth to do and the expected result. They believed the Report (Isa 53:1).

JOSEPH

Joseph knew who he was and why he was sold into slavery in Egypt. As a slave in Potiphar's house he was tempted through lust of the eyes, lust of the flesh and pride of life. At his most vulnerable moment, his master's wife said to him: '*come and lie with me.*' Joseph told Potiphar's wife: '*how can I do this and sin against God?*'

It takes those who know who they are, where they came from, what they are doing here and where they are going after this life to take correct decisions in life's daily battle. Joseph knew he was heir to the blessings of Abraham. He understood that yielding to the diverse lusts for a season would abort God's purpose for his life and put off-course God's plan for succeeding generations. Even when his brothers became remorseful in selling him to Ishmaelite merchants for twenty shekels of silver, Joseph comforted them by saying: "*... do not therefore be grieved or angry with yourselves because you sold me here; for God sent me before you to preserve life. And God sent me before you to preserve a posterity for you in the earth, and to save your lives by a great deliverance*" Gen 45: 5, 7).

ESTHER

Esther knew that her being beautiful, young and a slave in Babylon was not by accident. She knew her purpose in life was to preserve life even at the expense of her own life. "*If I perish, I perish*" was her response to the wicked plot of Haman.

JOHN THE BAPTIST

John the Baptist knew he was not the Christ but one sent ahead to lay the groundwork for Christ's earthly ministry. *Now this is the testimony of John, when the Jews sent priests and Levites from Jerusalem to ask him, "Who are you?" He confessed, and did not deny, but confessed, "I am not the Christ." He said: "I am 'the voice of one crying in the wilderness: make straight the way of the Lord' as the prophet Isaiah said"* (Jn 1:19-20, 23).

Do you have biblical answers to the Cardinal Questions of life? The original apostles knew who they were, what to do at every situation looking forward to the reward promised by the great 'Rewarder.'

THE APOSTLES IMITATED CHRIST

The Apostles knew who they were. They knew Jesus was the Messiah. They saw Him ascend into heaven and knew He would come back as He said. The Disciples expected the rapture to take place in their time. Their focus on the imminence of the rapture made them to be watchful. They were devoted to the things of God and earnestly longed to be with the Lord. They qualified as those who 'fell asleep.' The original eleven plus Paul died as martyrs.

HOW TO ANSWER THE CARDINAL QUESTIONS OF LIFE

The starting point is to be on the right path. Jesus is the way, the truth and the life. All other ways lead to perdition. To be on the right way you must be translated from death to life. Everyone born into this world carry a suspended death sentence. Jesus said: 'You are from beneath.' We all came from hell beneath having been conceived in sin and born in iniquity. With the new birth a change in origin and destination takes place.

In John chapter 3, Jesus told Nicodemus "*Most assuredly, I say to you, unless one is born again, he cannot see the kingdom of God.*" Again He said: "*Most assuredly, I say to you, unless one is born of water and the Spirit, he cannot enter the kingdom of God.*"

Seven Supernatural Acts of the Holy Spirit

When you surrender your life to Christ, the Holy Spirit performs some supernatural acts to confirm sonship of the penitent. These things are done or activated in the life to assure him or her of salvation.

1. Deliverance of spirit from satanic occupation on the basis of genuine confession of faith in the name of the Lord. Deliverance of spirit from ruler of darkness to change fatherhood.

2. Implantation of a Hypostatic Chip as one who is a son of God. The planting of Hypostatic Chip in the spirit subrogates the expelled demon, confirming the right of ownership and fatherhood of God.

3. Certification of name of Chip – which is already in the Lamb's Book of Life. Human names are not written in the Lamb's Book of life but taken note of by the Holy

Spirit for earthly transactional purposes only. Igniting of name of Hypostatic Chip in the Lamb's Book of Life as an indication that the 'son' of God has been accommodated in a human vessel and so allocated.

4. Sealing of believer in the Body of Christ – believer occupies a specific space in the mystical body of Christ described by Apostle Paul variously to be like a building, an army or a human body. Engrafting into the Body of Christ which is the first baptism is the seal of membership of being a child of God.

5. Ability to "see" certain things from God's perspective. Jn 3:3

6. Persistent prompting to share salvation testimony.

7. Check in the spirit when evil wants to manifest.

The Hypostatic Chip you received on regeneration is a mini-God from the heart of God. It is a life transformer with a growth path. The growth path is the narrow way to the strait gates of heaven. Your Hypostatic Chip must fuse with your innerman for you to enter heaven.

For a genuinely born again child of God, the Holy Spirit bears witness of sonship. This is followed immediately by manifestations of the new life. The following characteristics are easily noticeable in a changed life:

1. Witness of the Holy Spirit, similar to bootable software and the accompanying joy in the innerman. The Holy Spirit bears witness to the human spirit about the sonship of God. The message is transmitted from the Hypostatic Chip to the mind through the spirit. The clarity of the message depends on the state

of the spirit and the preparedness of the mind to receive divine information. The meaning may be unfamiliar or muffled as a result of the level of demonic bondage in the mind.

2. Salvation testimony. Eagerness to share the divine experience. Paul shared his salvation testimony wherever he had opportunity to preach the gospel message.

3. Immediate dropping of at least one vice.

4. Intense desire to know more about God evidenced by being in fellowship with the brethren.

5. Willingness to eat the flesh of Jesus and drink His blood by participating in the Lord's Supper and adhering to the Apostles' doctrine and fellowship.

6. Changed attitude towards sin.

7. Deep and heartfelt regret for falling into sin. A Christian does not commit sin; however, if overwhelmed by forces of darkness to fall into it, he or she may rebound through confession and washing by the blood of Jesus.

Growing in grace means the Hypostatic Chip which is a mini-Jesus resident inside of you must have full control of your spirit. Your spirit must have full control over your soul. Your soul must put your body under the suzerainty of the Hypostatic Chip through your innerman. This is sanctification (1 Thess 5:23). It is achieved through mind renewal (Rom 12:1-2).

The Hypostatic Chip, a word of God, is the bread of life. Life in the Chip must be downloaded through revelation, inspiration and illumination. The Word of God comprises logos and Rhema. The starting point is the written Word of God – the logos.

To be like Jesus, the Word of God, you must constantly:

1. Read the Word.

2. Hear the Word.

3. Study the Word.

4. Believe the Word.

5. Speak the Word.

6. Give the Word first place in your life.

7. Memorize the Word of God.

8. Meditate on the Word.

9. Know the Word, that is, where it is written in the Bible.

10. Be a doer of the Word, especially when the revelation is person-specific.

11. Tremble at the Word by having reverential fear of God.

12. Eat the Word symbolically through the ordinance of Holy Communion.

13. Encounter the Word made flesh in one of His many manifestations by desiring to be baptized in the Holy Spirit and by fire.

14. Preach the Word by sharing your salvation testimony, witnessing to the unsaved and by being the epistle that people can read and believe in the Lord Jesus Christ.

In addition, the revealed will of God should be adhered to with reverential fear of God. In this context, fear does not mean being afraid of God. On the contrary, God has not given us the spirit of fear but of power, and of love, and of a sound mind. Fear is Satan's property and it brings torment. To fear God means to acknowledge His almightiness; He has the power to do what He says He will do. Thus, the fear of the Lord means to love Him so wholeheartedly that you strive even to the point of death not to do anything that could dishonour the LORD. It is marked by obedience and willingness to do the will of God regardless of cost.

13

CHRIST-LIKENESS

*Behold what manner of love the Father has
bestowed on us, that we should be called children of God!
Therefore the world does not know us, because it did not know
Him. Beloved, now we are children of God; and it has not yet
been revealed what we shall be, but we know that when He is
revealed, we shall be like Him, for we shall see Him as He is.
And everyone who has this hope in Him purifies himself,
just as He is pure.*
1 Jn 3:1-3

FIRSTFRUITS OF THE SPIRIT

It is not tedious to reiterate that money is needed to acquire things of value; however, material things do not guarantee happiness in life. Mention has been made that it is possible for a person to have money and still be poor in spirit, soul and body. Clearly, a person's life does not consist in the abundance of the things the person has. However, if you do not have money's worth in material things and tradable assets you cannot have treasure in heaven. Investment precedes reward. Although spiritual treasure is more important than physical treasure, you need both to make impact in this life and in the one to come. Everybody has time and talents to invest in God's kingdom. Ascertaining who you are and why you are here is the starting point.

Fulfilling one's destiny is what God counts as success. Adhering to the principles of money, investment and savings ensure the availability of money for destiny fulfillment. Putting hope on money rather than God to solve pilgrimage challenges is an effort in futility. Money will fail, governments will collapse and the cities of the world will one day be buried in the ground (2 Pet 3:10). Integrity and character are more valuable assets than money and material things. True success is to have enough money for the Great commission and divine power to actualize it.

Jesus came from heaven above. The posterity of Adam and Eve came from hell beneath. The starting point of being like Jesus is to be translated from death to life. Implantation of Hypostatic Chip is evidence of eternal life. This is the new birth. Jesus fulfilled the first phase of his assignment in His first coming. The second phase cannot begin unless the Lord is united with His Body, the church in heaven. Prophesied second coming signs have been fulfilled. Nothing else can take place until the church is evacuated to heaven. Seven years after the rapture Jesus with His saints and holy angels will return to earth to begin a series of activities culminating in the establishment of the literal kingdom of God on earth.

MAKE MARRIAGE HONOURABLE

Sex is good; God made it good but it can be avoided with desirable time and eternal benefits. For those who have or can acquire the gift of celibacy marriage is an avoidable option. In this tail end of the endtime single status is better than marital entanglement especially if marriage is unrelated to one's destiny.

Apostle Paul, one of the most successful followers of Christ, embraced the single status. There is no joy as pleasurable as being in the presence of God and doing His will.

POWER IS A GIFT

Power is needed to solve problems. Real power resides in God: it is downloadable from Hypostatic Chips by those who hunger and thirst for righteousness. Power without divine control breeds anarchy. Baptism of the Holy Spirit bestows divine power. Baptism by fire enthrones the mind and character of Jesus on the recipient: it is total surrender to the will of Christ.

Inside every human being there is something neither money nor sex can satisfy. Money, sex and power in the bad ethical worldview can blind human eyes, weaken the power of visions and destroy destinies. Unsaved people spend most of their time thinking about money and sex and power for more money for limitless and ever-flowing sensual pleasure. Whereas to be perfect in God and inherit the promises of Christ is to spend most of one's time thinking about Christ's second coming, facilitate the unfulfilled part of the mandate of Jesus as led and to expect the rapture of the church to occur any time in one's lifetime.

EXPECTED END

Desiring things of value that give pleasure is a God-given capacity. There are things God wants us to desire and there are things God does not want us to desire. God wants His children to covet spiritual gifts; God does not want His children to covet what belongs to others. When your mind is focused on God the spirit of life operates to see things the way God sees them. A mind not focused on God is carnal being spiritually dead. A carnal mind cannot please God being linked with the law of sin and death.

Jesus is the Truth; truth can be seen only through regenerated human spirit. Desiring the truth is life; desiring the unfruitful works of darkness is sin unto death. If you desire money, sex and power to satisfy the longings of your fleshly passion you activate the law of sin and death in your blood – life is in the blood. If your desire lines up with the Word of God which is the mandate of Jesus you can have money, sex and power as part of the bargain. *"Delight yourself also in the Lord, and He shall give you the desires of your heart"* (Ps 37:4).

Before you can have good desire, however, you must know the will of God for your life. What is your destiny? Faith is to believe in your destiny. You must believe in yourself before you can have faith to believe in your destiny. You must have faith in yourself before you can have faith to believe in what you can or cannot do.

EXPECTATION OF RAPTURE

> Mt 24:36, 42, 44, 46-47
> **"But of that day and hour no one knows, not even the angels of heaven, but My Father only. Watch therefore, for you do not know what hour your Lord**

is coming. Therefore you also be ready, for the Son of Man is coming at an hour you do not expect. Blessed is that servant whom his master, when he comes, will find so doing. Assuredly, I say to you that he will make him ruler over all his goods."

Many believers have resigned from expecting the return of the Lord using as excuse Mt 24:36. They forget that when Jesus made that statement He had not been glorified, but now He has been glorified seating at the right hand of God Almighty awaiting the fullness of His Body. The same Bible says: "*Let this mind be in you, which was also in Christ Jesus*" (Phil 2:5). Those who have the mind of Christ are truly one with Him; they will know within a short space of time when the rapture will take place. Rapture will not overtake every believer by surprise. A privileged few will know something about the event just like Simeon, Anna, Elizabeth and John the Baptist knew in advance about the first coming of Christ.

Mature Christians will have an idea of the imminence of the event. Believers who qualify to participate in the rapture may not know the day or hour but will have an inner witness in their spirit about the sounding of the last trumpet. They will know the times and the seasons according to 1 Thess 5:1. If you do not know the times and the seasons you may still participate in the rapture but you are not likely to be part of the bride of Christ.

The Lord knows the harm it would cause saints in human flesh to know the day and hour of His coming but those who are knowledgeable of endtime events will not abuse the privilege but rather comfort and encourage those in Christ to look up to the heavens for their final redemption as they see the day approaching. Mature believers whose lifestyle reflects expectation of the return of the Lord have unique characteristics:

1. **Their orientation on life and living is focused on desire for the return of Jesus.** *"For our citizenship is in heaven, from which we also eagerly wait for the Savior, the Lord Jesus Christ, who will transform our lowly body that it may be conformed to His glorious body, according to the working by which He is able even to subdue all things to Himself"* (Phil 3:20-21).

2. **They see the world of men the way God sees it, corrupt, full of wickedness and ready for judgment and distance themselves from worldly pursuits.** *"For the grace of God that brings salvation has appeared to all men, teaching us that, denying ungodliness and worldly lusts, we should live soberly, righteously, and godly in the present age, looking for the blessed hope and glorious appearing of our great God and Savior Jesus Christ, who gave Himself for us, that He might redeem us from every lawless deed and purify for Himself His own special people, zealous for good works"* (Titus 2:11-14).

3. **Followers of Christ know that in His first advent Jesus came into the world as the Lamb of God to offer His life a ransom for many but in His second coming Jesus will come as the judge of the dead and the living.** *"Therefore, since all these things will be dissolved, what manner of persons ought you to be in holy conduct and godliness, looking for and hastening the coming of the day of God, because of which the heavens will be dissolved, being on fire, and the elements will melt with fervent heat? Nevertheless we, according to His promise,*

look for new heavens and a new earth in which righteousness dwells. Therefore, beloved, looking forward to these things, be diligent to be found by Him in peace, without spot and blameless" (Pet 3:11-14).

4. **They are like brides preparing for their wedding.** *"Beloved, now we are children of God; and it has not yet been revealed what we shall be, but we know that when He is revealed, we shall be like Him, for we shall see Him as He is. And everyone who has this hope in Him purifies himself, just as He is pure"* (1 Jn 3:2-3).

5. **Their evangelistic fervor reflects the way they zealously distribute their 'wedding invitation' witnessing to the lost and strengthening the weak in Christ.** *"So Christ was offered once to bear the sins of many. To those who eagerly wait for Him He will appear a second time, apart from sin, for salvation"* (Heb 9:28).

6. **They are more heaven-conscious than those who are living according to the dictates of the world system.** *"Not forsaking the assembling of ourselves together, as is the manner of some, but exhorting one another, and so much the more as you see the Day approaching"* (Heb 10:25).

7. **They are desirous of meeting the Lord just as a bride and groom are desirous of, and expectant of, their wedding day and the accompanying ceremonies.** *"For yet a little while, and He who is coming will come and will not tarry"* (Heb 10:37).

8. **Their attitude to money and wealth accumulation is guided by building eternal heritage in heaven.** *"That the genuineness of your faith, being much more*

precious than gold that perishes, though it is tested by fire, may be found to praise, honor, and glory at the revelation of Jesus Christ" (1 Pet 1:7).

9. **They experience 'birth pangs' signaling the approaching sound of the trumpet for the rapture of the church.** *"So that you come short in no gift, eagerly waiting for the revelation of our Lord Jesus Christ, who will also confirm you to the end, that you may be blameless in the day of our Lord Jesus Christ"* (1 Cor 1:7-8)

10. **Like the original apostles they are daily expecting the return of the Lord.** *"For as often as you eat this bread and drink this cup, you proclaim the Lord's death till He comes"* (1 Cor 11:26).

11. **Their earnest desire is to participate in the rapture as living saints.** *"Therefore be patient, brethren, until the coming of the Lord. See how the farmer waits for the precious fruit of the earth, waiting patiently for it until it receives the early and latter rain. You also be patient. Establish your hearts, for the coming of the Lord is at hand"* (Jam 5:7-8).

12. **They are like the sons of Issachar who had understanding of the times, to know what Israel ought to do per time.** *"But of the times and the seasons, brethren, ye have no need that I write unto you. ... But ye, brethren, are not in darkness, that that day should overtake you as a thief. Ye are all the children of light, and the children of the day: we are not of the night, nor of darkness. Therefore let us not sleep, as do others; but let us watch and be sober"* (1 Thess 5:1-6).

The original Apostles followed Jesus. So did Mary Magdalene and the other women who witnessed His passion from Galilee to Golgotha and continued to the Upper Room. They all had the mind of Christ and followed Jesus to the end of their lives.

To have the mind of Christ is to be like Him – to anticipate His next move and be in expectation. Those who followed Jesus to the end expected the second coming of Christ, to wit rapture, to occur in their lifetime.

Expectation of rapture is the earnest of followership of Christ. When we see the Lord Jesus Christ on rapture day we shall be like Him for we shall see Him in His glorified state. *"And everyone who has this hope in Him purifies himself, just as He is pure."* That is how to be Christ-like.

14

HOLY SPIRIT-CONTROLLED LIFE

But when the kindness and the love of God Our Savior toward man appeared, not by works of righteousness which we have done, but according to His mercy He saved us, through the washing of regeneration and renewing of the Holy Spirit, whom He poured out on us abundantly through Jesus Christ our Savior, that having been justified by His grace we should become heirs according to the hope of eternal life. If we live in the Spirit, let us also walk in the Spirit. For as many as are led by the Spirit of God, these are sons of God.
Titus 3:4-7; Gal 5:25; Eph 8:14

THE NEEDFUL THING

At the beginning of this book, we said that human destiny is embedded in every individual's Hypostatic Chip. The Chip does not become operational in man until implanted and activated at the point of regeneration. Hence, destiny fulfillment is a non-issue for those who have not received the new life that is in Christ Jesus. We cannot overemphasize the need for sinners to repent and be born again. For the saved, growth dictated by the Hypostatic Chip brings about destiny fulfillment and the promised *"future and a hope"* (Jer 29:11). It is the only guarantee for success in this life.

Thus, God has set standards for everything and everyone in the visible and invisible realm. A person's destiny is the standard set for him or her. God's standards specify the way things should be done at any point in time. Man has no discretion in setting, improving, revising or modernizing a standard set by God for him or her. Everyone has God-given ability to fulfill his or her destiny on earth. That accounts for the fact that human achievement without God is useless in destiny fulfillment.

Jesus Christ is the epitome of God's standards. Jesus conducted His earthly ministry totally in accordance with God's standards in the power of the Holy Spirit. He said: *"I can of Myself do nothing. As I hear, I judge; and My judgment is righteous, because I do not seek My own will but the will of the Father who sent Me"* Jn 5:30). Then Jesus said to them, *"When you lift up the Son of Man, then you will know that I am He, and that I do nothing of Myself; but as My Father taught Me, I speak these things"* (Jn 8:28).

For the standards God has set, the Holy Spirit helps those mindful of obeying them to meet the prescribed requirement. Everyone born of God has a Hypostatic Chip implanted in him or her. The purpose of the Chip, which is also known as the Incorruptible Seed, is to transform a born again Christian to become like Christ. Hypostatic growth means meeting the specific standards set for everyone. This is how a destiny can be fulfilled. It brings great rewards in time and eternity.

Conversely, it is unprofitable to do things according to standards based on culture, other peoples' opinion or what has always been done. Ignorance of divine standards is responsible for the prevalence of the 'traditions of the fathers' and for operating with double or no standards at all. It is profitable therefore to allow the Hypostatic Chip imprint Christ in the spirit and soul of the recipient. This is what it means to be led on daily basis by the Holy Spirit.

May the grace of our Lord Jesus Christ, the love of God and the fellowship of the Holy Spirit be with you, activate goodness and mercy to follow you all the days of your life and make you eligible to be raptured when the church will be evacuated to heaven, in Jesus name, Amen.

THE MARANATHA PROJECT (TMP)
Heralding The Second Coming Of Christ

TMP is about the concluding aspects of the mandate of Jesus and the final destination of human beings. It is also a compendium in various formats of revelations on events that are about to take place starting with the rapture of the church to the destruction of God's enemies at the Battle of Gog and Magog.

God's mandate to Jesus involves two comings to earth, three distinct activities spanning two dispensations with three finishing points. Designed to dovetail that mandate, the Project is about making decisions that determine eligibility for participation in the rapture of the church, which is the next event in God's prophetic calendar. It is about eternal life in contrast with eternal death, heaven and hell, abundant life or misery in time and eternity.

TMP resources are designed as an endtime strategic battle manual and guide along the narrow pathway to heaven's strait gate for Christians who desire to participate in the evacuation of the Church to heaven. The presentation in books of several volumes and other formats is the unveiling of the sequence of events when Jesus Christ returns to earth to complete His divine assignment that began with His incarnation.

TMP was birthed through what I received from the Lord over a period of seven years of waiting on Him. The ministry provides a prophetic support to believers to be part of the second and final aspects of the mandate of Jesus. Information about the ministry as well as books originating from The **MARANATHA** *Project* can be obtained from our website.

www.themaranathaproject.com

TMP BOOKS

The following is a brief description of Phase One titles:

JESUS IS COMING SOON: *Prepare For Judgment*
In His First Advent, Jesus came as the Lamb of God to seek and save lost mankind. His Second Coming is to judge the living and the dead and re-establish God's Kingdom on earth. Nobody can enter heaven unprepared. Those who fail to plan to live with Jesus in the New Jerusalem may transit to the New Earth or spend eternity in the lake of fire prepared for Satan and his followers. This book will help you prepare to meet your Maker in His gracious benevolence and avoid the calamitous tragedy that awaits unrepentant humanity after the rapture of the Church. Jesus is coming soon; be ready to meet Him in peace!

HEAVEN: *Twelve Imperatives For Entry*
God and His created beings will soon begin to relocate to one of three destinations starting with the rapture of the Church, which is imminent. This book focuses on human preparations to be equipped to dwell with God forever. It highlights seven requirements for permanent union with Christ, three electives to fulfill destiny on earth in order to occupy pre-ordained position in heaven and two options for those left behind after the rapture who desire a place in God's eternal kingdom. Ours is the terminal generation that will witness the evacuation of rapture-ready members of the Body of Christ to meet the Lord in the air. This book dwells extensively on eligibility criteria for those desiring to participate in the rapture of the church.

MARRIAGE: *An Exposition On Christian Marital Relationship*
Marital relationship is like a Cross; the vertical connects God upwards or binds with Satan downwards. The horizontal is human to human, pointing diametrically to godly or ungodly union. Marriage defines interaction with fellow human beings as well as spirit beings with consequences that lead to final eternal destination. The abundant life Jesus brought is designed for those in marital relationship with the Lord. In this life it means to be betrothed to Christ and abiding in Him. The Christian's ultimate hope is to be a Bride at the Marriage of the Lamb in heaven.

TITHES AND OFFERINGS: *Storing Treasures In Heaven*
The practice of tithing according to the Law of Moses in the New Testament Church falls short of new covenant standards for storing treasures in heaven. Besides, it has other avoidable repercussions. This book is an insightful revelation on the biblical method of using our time, talents and wealth to acquire true riches, which are spiritual bestowals of faith for fruitfulness in expediting the mandate of Jesus and for the purpose of attaining preordained position in heaven after this life.

MONEY, SEX & POWER: *Imitating Jesus Christ*
To be tempted is not evil; yielding to it is. Jesus was tempted on all points yet without sin. To imitate Him is to see life. Most people spend most of their time thinking about money and pleasure and power for more money for limitless sensual gratification. It is a vicious circle. Jesus' lifestyle on earth is the standard of God: everything He said and did was according to what was written about Him in the Scroll of the Book. There is a scroll in every believer's Hypostatic Chip that delimits earthly conduct. The Lord Jesus Christ who has given us power to follow His perfect example will one day judge the desires, imaginations and conduct of the dead and the living for eternal reward or punishment. This book teaches how to imitate Jesus in living God's kingdom lifestyle in this present evil world without being distracted by the allurement of "the three musketeers" money, sex and power.

DIVORCE & REMARRIAGE: *What The Bible Teaches*
Marriage is good but a defiled bed is a veritable ground for wickedness. Are there marriages not joined by God? Is marriage compulsory for every believer? God hates divorce in human marriage but does He punish the innocent with the guilty party? Are there circumstances in which God permits Christian divorce and remarriage? Ensnaring tendencies in marital unions are widespread and can lead untaught and laisser-faire Christians into perdition. There are destinies that cannot be fulfilled without dissolving ungodly marital relationships - human and spiritual. This book is a companion to, and complements, *MARRIAGE: An Exposition of Christian Marital Relationship.* It highlights what the Bible teaches on marriage divorce and remarriage.

PROSPERITY OF THE RIGHTEOUS: *Good Journey Through Life*
Very often, human perspective of prosperity is the accumulation of material things whereas God's perspective of prosperity has to do with what was written before the foundation of the world in every individual's Hypostatic Chip. Righteous prosperity is to have a good passage through earthly life by fulfilling destiny, create and use wealth to store eternal

treasures in heaven and qualify for church rapture as a sleeping or living saint. Earthly rewards are not bad, but greater and eternal rewards are reserved in heaven for those who use in this life their time, talents and material resources for the benefit of God's children and His kingdom. This is the righteous prosperity expounded in this book.

RAPTURE OF THE CHURCH: *Ten Reasons For Delay*
In His wisdom the day and hour of the rapture of the church God has chosen not to disclose to anyone; but not so with the times and seasons. It is plausible to assume that without the intense satanic opposition experienced by the church hitherto, the rapture probably would have taken place already. The first coming of Jesus Christ was delayed by generations owing to Judah's indiscretion with Tamar his daughter-in-law. In the same vein, some contemporary happenings in this end time church have the capacity for causing delay in the return of the Lord. Here are ten of such events.

THREE ETERNAL DESTINATIONS: *Mankind's Final Abode*
Every human being has eternal existence, but not everyone has eternal life. Everybody has three component parts: outward personality, inward personality and a controlling spirit. Your body is dust; your controlling Hypostatic Chip or demon must return to base but the real you comprising spirit and soul has three eternal destinations: New Jerusalem, New Earth or the Lake of Fire. Where you will spend eternity depends on the decisions you make or fail to make in this life. This book shows you the roadmap to New Jerusalem.

CHRIST'S SECOND COMING: *How To Prepare For Rapture*
The greatest Christian hope is expectation of the return of the Lord Jesus Christ, which will begin with the evacuation of sleeping and living saints to heaven before judgment begins. Since rapture is the starting point, it is the duty of living saints to be ready for the event. Although the day and hour of church rapture is secret, living saints who are in a state of watchfulness, readiness and fruitful occupation of the land will not be taken unawares by the imminence of the event. Here are ten biblical imperatives for any saint who genuinely desires to be fully prepared for the rapture and second coming of Christ.

MARITAL RELATIONSHIPS: *Uprooting Troublers of Marriage*
Human marriage creates troubles in this life. These 'normal' problems can easily be dealt with when couples work diligently to make their marriage work. There are 'abnormal' troubles, inherited or self-inflicted, that create turbulence in marriage. They must be identified and

uprooted before any marriage can serve the purpose of God and man. For those already married or intending to marry, this book is a spiritual warfare manual for grappling with manmade problems in mismatched marriages. A godly marriage can be a blessing and not a curse to the spouse and society when abnormal situations in marriage are adequately dealt with in order to serve God's purpose. This book is a do-it-yourself manual.

SUCCESS THAT COUNTS WITH GOD: *Fulfilling Divine Destiny*

Inside every human being there is a void material possession, creative achievement and human accolade cannot satisfy. That is why success in life does not depend on the abundance of one's material wealth, pleasurable privileges and bestowal of honors but on perfect union of human spirit, soul and body with the implanted Hypostatic Chip, an excision from the heart of God, the divine agency designed to ignite passion for things of eternal value in willing mankind. Not all success is good success. Therefore, this volume is a handbook on how to run the race of life purposefully in order to succeed where it really matters with God.

MATERIAL PROSPERITY DOCTRINE: *The Hidden Agenda*

In the early church the doctrine of circumcision was craftily introduced to derail the apostolic commission of witnessing Christ to the utmost ends of the earth. In the contemporary church, the doctrine of material prosperity has crept in with a hidden agenda.

The next event in God's Prophetic Calendar is the rapture of the church. For there to be an endtime revival to prepare the Body of Christ for the event the church must rise to checkmate the intrusion of this divisive and destructive doctrine and return to the old narrow path as did the original Apostles. It is possible!

WISDOM IS PROFITABLE TO DIRECT: *Nuggets On Life's Issues*

Jesus is the wisdom of God. The Final Word is inclusion in the Priesthood by the Lord Jesus Christ who will establish the literal kingdom of God on earth at His second coming. This book is a compilation of revealed truth received over a period of two decades. Classified as axioms, frontlets and nuggets, it covers areas of interest to the eschatological community and to those mindful of the second coming of Christ and the consequences of that coming.

About The Author

Collins Enyeribe is the President of Evangelical Fellowship Institute Inc., a ministry dedicated to the dissemination of endtime doctrine. He has a first degree in Business Administration from the University of Nigeria, and belongs to many professional bodies including the Institute of Chartered Accountants of Nigeria, as a fellow. He worked in a development bank for almost three decades before going into full-time ministry as a prophetic teacher, preacher of the word of God and relationship counselor.

He is the coordinator of *Focus On The Rapture* seminars where issues relating to the second coming of Christ and eligibility for participation in the rapture of the Church are deliberated upon in the light of Bible prophecies and current events. As a relationship counselor, he conducts *Focus On Marriage* workshops that deal with practical aspects of human and spiritual relationships.

FEEDBACK
The author would like to know if
THE *MARANATHA* PROJECT
as a Christian resource has made any
positive impact or helped in any way in
your work and walk with the Lord.

E-mail comments to:
collinsenyeribe@gmail.com.
Tel: 234: 0814-650-5012 (text only)
Website: www.evangelicalfellowshipinstitute.org